FROM BASELINE TO BASELINE, B-BALL HAS NEVER BEEN SO WACKY!

Q Why were New Jersey Nets fans waving dollar bills in the stands every time Chris Dudley went to the free throw line on April 14, 1990?
            (see chapter on *Shooting Most Foul*)

Q What college showboat would attempt shots from his knees during games?
            (see chapter on *Odd Balls*)

Q What did Englewood Cliffs College do after it lost a game by 143 points?
            (see chapter on *The Bottom of the Barrel*)

Q What Utah Jazz coach, after seeing his team getting trounced by the Los Angeles Lakers, went across the street for a sandwich during the middle of the fourth quarter?
            (see chapter on *Headless Coaches*)

Q Why is Bethesda, Maryland, attorney Robin Ficker universally detested by visiting NBA teams?
            (see chapter on *Booing the Boosters*)

Books by Bruce Nash and Allan Zullo

The Baseball Hall of Shame™
The Baseball Hall of Shame™ 2
The Baseball Hall of Shame™ 3
The Baseball Hall of Shame™ 4
Baseball Confidential™   .
The Football Hall of Shame™
The Football Hall of Shame™ 2
The Golf Hall of Shame™
The Sports Hall of Shame™
The Basketball Hall of Shame™

Published by POCKET BOOKS

Most Pocket Books are available at special quantity discounts for bulk purchases for sales promotions, premiums or fund raising. Special books or book excerpts can also be created to fit specific needs.

For details write the office of the Vice President of Special Markets, Pocket Books, 1230 Avenue of the Americas, New York, New York 10020.

THE
BASKETBALL
HALL OF SHAME™

BRUCE NASH and ALLAN ZULLO

BERNIE WARD, CURATOR

POCKET BOOKS

New York   London   Toronto   Sydney   Tokyo   Singapore

An *Original* Publication of Pocket Books

POCKET BOOKS, a division of Simon & Schuster Inc.
1230 Avenue of the Americas, New York, NY 10020

Nash, Bruce M.
  The basketball hall of shame / Bruce Nash and Allan Zullo.
    p.   cm.
  ISBN: 0-671-69414-6 : $9.00
  1. Basketball—United States—Anecdotes.   2. Basketball—United
States—Humor.   I. Title.
GV885.7.N35   1991
796.323'0973—dc20   91-22996
                                                                          CIP

First Pocket Books trade paperback printing December 1991

10 9 8 7 6 5 4 3 2 1

THE BASKETBALL HALL OF SHAME is a
trademark of Nash and Zullo Productions, Inc.

To Steve Wohl, for leading me to my field of dreams so I could have one last game of catch with my dad.

—B.N.

To my good friend Nick Griffis, who stands tall both on and off the basketball court.

—A.Z.

ACKNOWLEDGMENTS

We wish to thank all the fans, players, coaches, and sportswriters who contributed nominations.

We are especially grateful to those players past and present who shared a few laughs as they recounted the inglorious moments that earned them a place in The Basketball Hall of SHAME.

This book couldn't have been completed without the assistance and cooperation of the Naismith Memorial Basketball Hall of Fame in Springfield, Massachusetts. We appreciate the help and guidance of Wayne Patterson, the Hall of Fame's research specialist, and to J. Mark Sweeney, researcher at the Library of Congress.

Special thanks go to: Lee Baker, Jake Bethany, Joe Cook, Jim Drucker, Tim Dutton, Steve Dykes, Julie Fie, Kenneth Goodwin, Sr., Bill Himmelman, Alan Karpick, Janet Knott, Lenn Margolis, Kevin McKinney, Ernie Salvatore, Ray Sanchez, Bud Vander Veer, and Eric Whittington.

Our lineup wouldn't be complete without our teammates in life, Sophie Nash and Kathy Zullo.

CONTENTS

THE
BASKETBALL
HALL OF SHAME™

THE OPENING TIP

Ever since December, 1891, when Dr. James Naismith first instructed students to toss a soccer ball into two peach baskets fastened to the gymnasium balcony at Springfield College, basketball has enjoyed many of the sports world's most wonderful moments. And its most blunderful.

We covered some of the game's more outrageous, rip-roaring gaffes in a chapter in The Sports Hall of Shame, *published in 1987. But we would be derelict in our duties as chroniclers of shame if we didn't devote an entire book to basketball—the hottest spectator team sport in America today. And what better time to celebrate the funny side of hoops than on the game's 100th birthday.*

Fortunately for all of us fans who love to laugh, college and pro basketball provide a never-ending supply of embarrassingly hilarious incidents. These funny foul-ups happen to coaches, rookies, and veterans. Even superstars.

We've received hundreds of nominations from readers and from fans whom we met on our cross-country travels to basketball arenas. From the locker rooms to the practice floors, players and coaches have tipped us off to other zany stories of unforgettable blunders. Many more wacky incidents surfaced when we spent days digging through the archives at the Naismith Memorial Basketball Hall of Fame in Springfield, Massachusetts.

Just what does it mean to be in The Basketball Hall of SHAME? It's a special recognition of a moment we can all identify with— and laugh about—because each of us has screwed up at one time or another.

Hall of Famers are no exception. For example, Rick Barry twice dashed off the court during games with a towel wrapped around him—after his pants split open. "Those definitely were my two most embarrassing moments in basketball," Barry confessed.

Many former players who had long been forgotten were delighted to hear they had been selected for induction. At least, they reasoned, they would be remembered for something, even if it was just an inglorious but funny moment.

For instance, we tracked down one of the NBA's all-time great flakes, Jim Barnett. When told he had made it into The Basketball Hall of SHAME, Barnett said, "I finally found a place that will accept me. Now I know why I did all those nutty things."

The Basketball Hall of SHAME makes no distinction between a superstar like the Boston Celtics' Larry Bird and a backup like the Detroit Pistons' Scott Hastings. Both are all-star pranksters and Hall of Shamers. On sharing Hall of SHAME dishonors with Bird, Hastings said, "I've always felt I could compete with Larry Bird—maybe not on the basketball court, but it's nice to know I'm right up there alongside him in The Basketball Hall of SHAME."

You might notice two unusual things about this book—for a story that's included and for one that isn't.

For the first time ever in the Hall of SHAME series, we are including an encore presentation of a story that ran in one of our previous books. The incident, which was recalled in The Sports Hall of Shame, is the shame of shames in hoops history—when the United States basketball team was robbed of the gold medal by bumbling referees and a power-crazed courtside official during the 1972 Olympic Games. The travesty was so outrageous that we felt it was worth retelling in this book.

There is one player who has yet to reach the (sub)standards required for Hall of SHAME induction—the Chicago Bulls' future Hall of Famer Michael Jordan. Much to our dismay, the guy simply hasn't done anything shameful enough yet. However, before his fantastic career is over, we feel confident he will do something to make him a Hall of Shamer.

Meanwhile, basketball will continue to produce more hilarious happenings on and off the court. And we will continue to chronicle these zany moments of both the superstars and the bozos. As our motto says: "Fame and shame are part of the game."

THAT'S THE WAY THE ROOKIE CRUMBLES

Aspiring players dream about what their first game will be like. They see themselves as heroes who sink the game-winning basket or make the game-saving blocked shot. That's the fantasy. The reality is that rookies often embarrass themselves at the beginning of a career that can be a whole lot shorter than they had ever planned. For "The Most Inauspicious Debuts," The Basketball Hall of SHAME inducts the following:

EARVIN "MAGIC" JOHNSON
Guard ○ Los Angeles Lakers ○ Oct. 12, 1979

Never before or since have the Los Angeles Lakers bombarded fans and the press with as much hype over a new player as they did for rookie Magic Johnson.

But when the day of Johnson's greatly anticipated debut finally arrived, Magic conjured up a mortifying scene. He dashed onto the court for the very first time—and fell flat on his face!

It was an audacious beginning for the young superstar from Michigan State, whom the Lakers had touted as the greatest thing to happen to basketball since they cut the bottoms out of Dr. Naismith's peach baskets. The Lakers were promising fans there would be a "magical happening" in the Forum when Magic arrived for the 1979–80 season. Before the first-round draft pick had even stepped foot on an NBA court, his photo appeared in ads in Los Angeles and in other NBA cities, proclaiming the dawn of a new age. In fact, before preseason camp opened, Lakers coach Jack McKinney bragged, "The fans want excitement and we promised them excitement—magical excitement."

AP/Wide World Photos

On the day of Magic's debut, *Los Angeles Times* sportswriter Scott Ostler told his readers, "Magic has been entrusted with the controls of one of the world's most expensive and talented basketball teams. It's a lofty position. . . . Magic is, in many ways, one of a kind."

The buildup was so great that Johnson's first game was televised nationally. Hundreds of Lakers fans who wanted to see Magic's NBA debut in person traveled to San Diego where the Lakers were taking on the Clippers.

But that night, with eager fans packing the arena and hundreds of thousands watching at home, the Magic man launched his professional career by blowing his first trick.

Hoping to milk all the hype they could out of Johnson's debut, the Lakers arranged for Magic to lead the team onto the court for pregame warm-ups. A ball boy was assigned to feed the ball to Magic, who would dribble to the basket and dunk the first lay-up to open the season.

"I was really nervous and excited since it was my first game ever as a pro," recalled Johnson. "We came running out of the locker room tunnel and hit the court. I took the ball and as I was dribbling in for my first lay-up . . . Boom! . . . I fell right on my face. My warm-up pants had slipped down and I got all tangled up and tripped.

"I was so nervous that I must have forgotten to lace up my sweat pants tightly enough. I just stepped all over myself. When I got done tumbling, I looked up and saw that the whole team was standing around me and laughing at me. Then the crowd started laughing. All I could do was get up and grin about it."

Magic shook off his abashment and played a great game, scoring 26 points to lead the Lakers to a 103–102 victory. But to this day it's the pregame flop that Magic remembers most about his debut.

"Everybody was there to see me play in my first game," he recalled. "It was even on national television. And it turned out to be my most embarrassing moment."

SPENCER HAYWOOD

Forward ○ University of Detroit Titans ○ Nov. 30, 1968

Spencer Haywood's debut as a collegiate star was a smashing show-stopper. Literally.

Almost single-handedly, Haywood crushed Aquinas College by scoring 36 points, pulling down 31 rebounds—and, for good measure, smashing the backboard to smithereens with a monster jam.

Since there was no spare board in stock, and since the University of Detroit Titans were ahead by a whopping 65 points, the rest of the game was called off.

It was the future NBA all-star's first appearance in a major college game, although he had led the United States to victory in the Olympics the previous summer.

"The game was really a big event for me," recalled Haywood. "I was playing my first college game at home in front of all my family and friends. So it was a night when the adrenaline was really pumping."

With Haywood pointing the way, the Titans quickly ran away with the game. With his team's comfortable lead, the 6-foot, 8-inch forward decided to test one of his theories and entertain his hometown fans at the same time.

"I had been talking to one of my teammates about the possibility of dunking from behind the key," recalled Haywood. "We'd never seen it done before. But I knew I could get up high because during pregame warm-ups someone would climb up and put quarters on the top of the backboard. I could jump high enough from under the basket to take them off."

With six and a half minutes to play, Haywood got the chance to try the long-distance dunk on a Titan fast break. "I came downcourt and took off from behind the free throw line near the top of the key," said Haywood. "I felt like I was flying. I was looking right down on the basket. In fact, I was so high I scared myself."

A courageous Aquinas defender set himself to take a charge, only to watch in astonishment as the airborne Titan sailed right over the top of his head.

"I slammed the ball home," said Haywood. "The force of coming down from that height with such momentum was so great that the basket and board just exploded.

"I was just as shocked as anyone. No one had ever really destroyed a basket and backboard the way I demolished that one. Players like Darryl Dawkins who came along later and started breaking boards were really wimps. They did it by hanging or pulling on the rims. Not me. I came straight down on that basket and it went to pieces."

There were more than 10,000 witnesses to Haywood's thunderous dunk. But as the noise of falling glass died away, there was absolute silence in the huge arena. For several seconds, the stunned crowd held its breath.

"Then a low rumble started that kind of built to a huge roar," said Haywood. "It was like all those 10,000 people right on cue went 'Wow!' "

The officials considered charging Haywood with a technical for dunking (which was prohibited in college back then). But there were extenuating circumstances. Detroit was ahead 105–40, the backboard couldn't be replaced, and there was 6:31 left on the clock. So the refs made the only rational decision—they called an end to the game and Spencer Haywood's debut.

CHARLOTTE HORNETS
Oct. 14, 1988

The Charlotte Hornets lost their first game as an NBA expansion team partly because they were just itching to play.

The players were brand new. The uniforms were brand new. Even the jockstraps were brand new—and that's what sent the Hornets into a tailspin.

Nathaniel Butler/NBA Photos

"We went up to play the New Jersey Nets for our first exhibition game," recalled Charlotte trainer Terry Kofler. "The game was in Madison Square Garden and we were all hyped up about making a good showing in the big city.

"It turned out to be a disaster—thanks to those darn athletic supporters."

Kofler said that the Hornets' new teal, purple, and white designer uniforms were late coming from the manufacturer and didn't arrive until minutes before game time. The same was true for the new socks and jockstraps.

"Everything was still in boxes," Kofler explained. "We didn't have time to fit the uniforms properly. Some guys looked OK. But since the pants were pleated, they ballooned out on other players and they looked awful—like they were wearing bloomers."

In the rush to suit up, Kofler forgot one important task—making sure the new jockstraps were washed before handing them out.

"With certain brands of athletic supporters, you really have to launder them first," said Kofler. "If you don't, there's something in them that causes really intense itching—as bad as poison ivy on some guys. Unfortunately, we had one of those brands."

The Hornets squirmed their way through the first half, desperately trying not to scratch their privates in front of all those sophisticated New Yorkers. Players were turning to each other on the bench and saying, "Do you itch?" "Yeah, you too?" At halftime, they made a beeline for the locker room. Players ripped off their new uniforms, dropped the offending jockstraps, and began scratching at those aggravating itches.

"I'll have to say that for an expansion team, they showed remarkable unity," Kofler laughed. "To a man, they stood there naked from the waist down and scratched in unison."

Coach Dick Harter picked that moment to come into the locker room to deliver his first halftime speech. He did a double take as he saw a horde of Hornets frantically scratching at their crotches.

"I knew the first half had been bad," Harter admitted later. "But when I saw all those naked guys, I wondered, 'Are they thinking about going home?'"

After the players dumped the offending jockstraps in a heap, Kofler managed to get the new garments washed before the second half started. The Hornets' itchy condition definitely improved. Unfortunately, their play did not. Charlotte lost its first game 118–97.

KEEPING AN EYE ON HIS MAN

During a 1952 game with the Milwaukee Hawks, the Philadelphia Warriors' Paul Arizin had a field day, scoring 30 points in the first half.

At the break, Hawks coach Doxie Moore pulled aside his rookie center, Mel Hutchins, and said, "Get out there and watch Arizin closely."

Replied Hutchins, "I've been watching him, Coach. Isn't he just wonderful?"

KIKI VANDEWEGHE

Forward ○ Denver Nuggets ○ Jan. 23, 1981

If Kiki Vandeweghe's hometown debut had been a burlesque show, he would have gotten the hook in the first act.

In fact, the rookie played so poorly that his team, the Denver Nuggets, were lucky to lose by only five points to the Los Angeles Lakers.

"Most players, asked to choose a most memorable game, will pick one in which they scored a career-high in points, made a last-second winning shot, or won a championship," said Vandeweghe. "My selection is completely opposite. The low point came when I was with the Denver Nuggets and we played the Lakers at the Forum. This was the first time I had been back in the Los Angeles area to play since I had graduated from UCLA eight months earlier."

As a senior at UCLA, Vandeweghe had averaged 19.5 points per game, leading the Bruins into the NCAA championship game, which they lost to Louisville. He was then picked 11th overall in the 1980 draft and signed by Denver.

The highly touted rookie forward was excited about his first trip back to L.A. Of the 14,813 fans at the Forum, about a third were friends and family members who had turned out to cheer Vandeweghe's homecoming. Everyone expected a great performance from him. After all, he came from a family of overachievers. His dad, Ernie, was an outstanding player at Colgate and for the New York Knicks. His uncle, Mel Hutchins, was an NBA Rookie of the Year with the Knicks. His sister, Tauna, was an Olympic swimmer and his mother, Colleen, was a Miss America. The pressure was on Vandeweghe. He just had to be good.

He wasn't.

In one of the worst debuts ever, Vandeweghe missed his first 11 shots and finished with a disastrous 1-for-13 night from the floor. "I wanted to do well," he recalled. "I wasn't particularly nervous, but maybe I should have been. Maybe being too relaxed was my problem."

As a starter on the Nuggets, Vandeweghe played about 15 minutes in the first half. "For me, it was a wasted half," he said. "I missed all four of my field goal attempts and didn't score a point."

The third quarter was the same for him—no points. He not only couldn't get his shots to fall, he couldn't even get some of them to reach the basket. In a span of 30 seconds, the rookie had two shots jammed down his throat—one by Kareem Abdul-Jabbar and another by Jim Chones.

Finally, early in the fourth period, Vandeweghe broke his embarrassing scoring drought by sinking two free throws. His family didn't know whether to cheer him for making them or groan because that's all he had to show for more than three quarters of action.

Late in the game, Vandeweghe had the chance to redeem himself. He scored his one and only field goal and a free throw to give Denver a 105–103 lead with less than two minutes to play. But the Lakers quickly tied the score. Then, as Denver set up a play, Vandeweghe was called for traveling. L.A. quickly took advantage of the turnover and scored. Later, with just 33 seconds left in the game and Denver trailing by three points, Vandeweghe drove in for what appeared to be an easy lay-up. He blew it. The Lakers went on to beat the Nuggets 110–105.

"When you go back to your hometown, you want to do well," said Vandeweghe. "I was horrible. I was very upset and disappointed. Sometimes you have games when the ball just doesn't go in. But why did it have to be this one?"

CLEVELAND CAVALIERS   MIAMI HEAT
1970–71   1988–89

No teams now playing in the NBA had more shameful debuts than the Miami Heat and the Cleveland Cavaliers.

The Cavs paved the way to ignobility by losing their first 15 games; the Heat bettered that dubious mark by dropping their first 17 contests.

The teams picked up losses the way a junkyard dog picks up fleas. Their constant defeats captured the imagination of fans throughout the league who had their own names for the teams—the Cleveland Cadavers and the Miami Sleet (for their cold shooting).

The only bright spot for the Cavaliers during their stumbling start was that Coach Bill Fitch (shown in photo) somehow managed to maintain a sense of humor—a very sick one.

After their first road trip, in which they lost all seven of their games by an average of 17 points, Fitch said, "I feel like a guy who has lockjaw and seasickness at the same time."

As Cleveland's losses piled up without a win, Fitch muttered, "Sometimes you wake up in the morning and wish your parents had never met."

During their initial home stand, the Cavs clearly demonstrated why they were bottom of the barrel material. Trailing the Portland Trail Blazers by only three points late in the game, and with the fans praying for the first win, Fitch called a time-out and delivered a fiery, win-one-for-the-home-folks pep talk.

The Cavaliers charged back onto the court. Guard Bobby Lewis launched a long downcourt pass to teammate John Warren, who was streaking for the basket. Warren caught the pass in midstride and slammed home a bone-rattling, in-your-face dunk.

But nobody cheered. Warren had put the ball in the wrong basket! The blunder boosted Portland's lead to five points and snuffed out Cleveland's rally. The embarrassed Cavs lost again.

"I wasn't the only one who screwed up," said a humbled Warren. "Some of my teammates were right there beside me yelling for the ball themselves."

Back on the road again, the frustrated Fitch took to wandering the streets at night in search of answers. Before a game in San Francisco, a guard stopped Fitch at the back door to the Cow Palace. Fitch had no identification, so the guard refused to let him in. "I'm the Cleveland coach," insisted Fitch. "Who else would be sneaking through the back alleys alone at night?"

The guard let him in. But it probably would have been better if he hadn't. The Warriors handed the Cavaliers their 15th consecutive loss by a lopsided score of 109–74. Cleveland shot a frigid 23 percent from the field.

AP/Wide World Photos

During that second road trip, the Cavs also lost to the Philadelphia 76ers by 54 points. At the half, Cleveland was already 48 points behind. When Fitch returned to the court following halftime, he gave the peace sign to the Sixers coach as a friendly gesture of surrender. "He returned a slightly different gesture," recalled Fitch.

The Cavs finally got it right on their 16th attempt at a win when they beat the Portland Trail Blazers 105–103.

The game was so badly played that a Portland reporter wrote, "It was difficult to tell in Thursday night's game—which was played in comparative silence as if the 2,000 fans who came were watching a heart transplant rather than a sporting event—if Cleveland won it, or Portland lost it."

And Fitch later added, "It looked like the gamblers got to both teams."

But the Cavs were back in form and lost their next 11 games en route to a woeful 15–67 season. Lamented Fitch, "What this team needs is a chaplain, not a coach."

The Miami Heat needed all the prayers they could get to ease their suffering while they set the record for the all-time worst debut in NBA history.

As Miami's losses mounted, the streak endeared the Heat to fans across the country. Even David Letterman got into the act on his late-night TV show when he gave one of his infamous Top Ten Lists. Of the ten reasons why Yasir Arafat, head of the Palestine Liberation Organization, should be allowed into the United States, reason number seven was: "Arafat's three-point shooting could help the Heat win a game."

Pat Williams, general manager of the Orlando Magic, said the Heat were losing so frequently, "their mascot should be a Democrat."

After dropping their first 12 games, the Heat had a chance to break the jinx at home when they played the lowly Sacramento Kings. Heat co-owner Zev Buffman wore sneakers to the game so he could spring from his courtside seat onto the floor and "hug the whole team" when the final buzzer sounded. But Miami blew an 11-point fourth-quarter lead and lost 96–94. "We had victory staring us in the face and I guess it scared us," said dejected Heat backup center Scott Hastings.

When the Heat broke the record for the worst start after losing their 16th straight, Hastings didn't mope. Instead, he acted like a high school kid collecting yearbook signatures, imploring his teammates and coaches to sign the stat sheet. "I'm going to frame this," he said.

The Heat got no respect. During another defeat, Miami coach Ron Rothstein questioned a technical foul that referee Jim Capers had called on Hastings. "Tell me, Jim," said a frustrated Rothstein. "Would you call that technical on Magic Johnson?"

Capers indicated that he would have—and then called one on Rothstein for asking the question.

After his team recorded its 17th consecutive defeat, Rothstein admitted, "The worst thing I think about is—what else?—actually going zero and 82. You look at the schedule and think, well, who *are* we going to beat? And when?"

The answer came the next night. The Heat finally tasted victory when they "clobbered" the Los Angeles Clippers 89–88. Miami finished its first season with the same record as Cleveland did in its inaugural year: 15–67.

JOHN CARTY

Center ○ University of California Golden Bears ○ Feb. 7, 1988

John Carty made the foulest debut in college history.

While most players dream of scoring a point a minute, Carty lived a nightmare of committing a foul a minute. In his first start as a big-time college player, the University of California freshman was whistled for five fouls in five minutes.

In 1988, Arizona came into Berkeley ranked number one in all the polls. California coach Lou Campanelli didn't want his Golden Bears to wimp out against the powerful Wildcats. Since the 6-foot, 9-inch Carty had played so aggressively in practice, Campanelli decided to start the green freshman at center for the first time.

"All my family and friends were in the stands," recalled Carty. "It was supposed to be my big debut. It turned out to be my big embarrassment.

"I thought my job was to go in and rough people up, agitate them, and get Arizona in foul trouble. But I was just a stupid, 215-pound freshman trying to push the big guys around. It didn't work."

Carty was lightning quick—at picking up fouls. Spectators were still looking for their seats three minutes after tip-off when Carty collected his third personal. "The fouls were all in the paint," said Carty. "Most of them were for hammering guys when they were going through the middle trying to take a shot."

After the three quick fouls, Campanelli benched the frosh, but he put him back in the lineup to start the second half. Two minutes later, Carty returned to his seat after committing his fourth and fifth personals. Five fouls in five minutes of playing time.

"Even the coach was surprised to see me back on the bench so soon," laughed Carty. "He really expected me to last a little longer than that.

"I felt awful about fouling out so fast in my first game. But it was even more embarrassing when the story about the game came out in the newspaper the next day. The headline read: 'John Carty: If You Went to the Bathroom, You Probably Missed Him.' "

ODD BALLS

Every team has at least one—a player who's like a loose ball that bounces out of bounds. He's a relish-laden hot dog, a corny flake, a wild card whose big mouth or zany antics have triggered some of the craziest court scenes this side of a Manhattan night court on New Year's Eve. For "The Daffiest Characters in the Game," The Basketball Hall of SHAME inducts the following:

CHARLES BARKLEY

Forward ○ Auburn ○ 1981–84

No NBA superstar was kidded about the size and shape of his body while in college the way Charles Barkley was.

The 6 foot, 6 inch, 260 pound all star averaged more fan-inspired nicknames per season than he did points during his days as a star for Auburn.

Before every college game, rival Southeastern Conference fans greeted him with jibes about his weight—which hovered from 275 to 300 pounds—and his legendary yen for pizza.

Among the more creative monikers that college fans gave Barkley were the Love Boat, Food World, the Bread Truck, the Crisco Kid, Tons of Fun, the Leaning Tower of Pizza, Boy Gorge, the Goodtime Blimp, and the one that followed him to the NBA—the Round Mound of Rebound.

At Louisiana State University, where the fans were even nastier, Barkley was known simply as the Fat Boy.

Next to basketball, Barkley's passion during his college days at Auburn centered on pizza. His appetite for pizza was so gigantic that he almost single-handedly kept a Domino's franchise near campus from going under.

One of the pizza delivery outlets opened a few blocks from Barkley's apartment, explained John Lewandowski, the sports information director at the university. "Every night, just like clockwork, Domino's would get a call," said Lewandowski. "It was Barkley. All he said was, 'This is Charles,' and the guy who took the call would answer, 'We'll be right there.'

"He didn't even have to place an order. They automatically knew what to fix and where to deliver it. A few minutes later, two large-size pizzas arrived just for Barkley. The people at Domino's still claim that Barkley was the only thing that kept them in business when they first opened."

When fans at other SEC schools learned of Barkley's prodigious fondness for pizza, they often taunted him with visions of his favorite snack during games.

At Kentucky, most of the spectators in the student section waved empty Domino's boxes whenever Auburn visited Lexington. The empty containers sailed out of the stands like oversized square Frisbees as Barkley trotted onto the floor during player introductions.

Another time, while the Auburn star was going through warm-ups before a game at Tennessee, a fan dressed up in a Domino's uniform approached Barkley to take his order. Before the Leaning Tower of Pizza could respond, the fan was ushered off the floor.

LSU supporters came up with the topper. They actually had Domino's deliver a large, piping-hot pizza to Barkley at courtside during a game. "Charles never got his hands on it though," recalled Lewandowski. "He probably wanted to."

When he wasn't eating pizza, Barkley was gorging on ice cream—by the bucket.

For a trip to play the University of Georgia in Athens, Barkley got on the team bus carrying a tub of ice cream. "It wasn't one of those little gallon cartons most people take home," recalled Lewandowski. "I'm talking about one of those industrial-sized drums you find in an ice cream store. He ate the whole thing before we got to Athens."

Despite an average playing weight of 280 pounds, Barkley led the SEC in rebounding for three years. "But nobody knew it," he once complained. "I was just a fat guy who could play basketball well."

The Philadelphia 76ers took him fifth in the college draft but were less than pleased when he reported at nearly 300 pounds. Chided Pat Williams, who was general manager at the time, "He's so fat that his bathtub has stretch marks."

Barkley managed to shed about 40 pounds to get to his NBA playing weight. When asked how he did it, Barkley replied, "I cut down to six meals a day."

QUINTIN DAILEY

Guard ○ Chicago Bulls ○ March 20, 1985

There's a time and place to eat. Quintin Dailey chose the bench—during a game!

The 6-foot, 2-inch, 215-pound reserve guard worked up quite a powerful appetite riding the Bulls' bench during a 1985 game against the San Antonio Spurs. Midway through the third period, Dailey's hunger pangs were working overtime. He just had to fill his belly . . . right now.

So the porky player signaled for the ball boy to join him at the end of the Chicago bench. After a whispered conference, the ball boy approached the press table and began soliciting donations from reporters covering the game.

After the ball boy explained that Dailey was famished and pining for pizza, one of the incredulous reporters loaned him five bucks. The ball boy took off for the concession stand and minutes later returned with a warm piece of pizza and gave it to Dailey.

And right there, in front of his teammates and a Chicago Stadium crowd, Dailey wolfed down the pizza!

But a single slice wasn't enough to satisfy the hungry Bull. Throughout the quarter, he made the gofer go back for more—like nachos, a bag of popcorn, and a soft drink.

"I noticed the kid at the press table asking for money for food," recalled Tim Hallam, the Bulls' public relations official. "I didn't pay much attention until I saw him delivering takeout to Quintin down on the bench. I couldn't believe my eyes, but there he was chowing down while the game was going on."

Kevin Loughery, who was coaching the Bulls at the time, said Dailey's courtside pig-out left him speechless—and angry enough to eventually trade him.

"We were struggling just to make the play-offs," recalled Loughery. "I remember glancing over just when Quintin was putting away a slice of pizza. I thought to myself, 'No, I really didn't see that.'"

Some action on the court drew Loughery's attention back to the game. "A little later, I noticed he was eating again," said Loughery. "I don't know what it was, but it sure seemed like he was stuffing his face. What could I say? 'Give me a bite'?"

RICK BARRY

Forward ○ San Francisco Warriors ○ April 12, 1967

One of Rick Barry's greatest games was also his most humbling.

Before shooting out the lights in a big playoff game, he shot off his mouth—and angered fans, who pelted him with candy bars, eggs, tomatoes, beer, and hot dogs during the contest. Barry never lost his cool. Unfortunately, he lost something else—his pants.

Throughout his career, Barry was as well known for his hot temper as he was for his hot hand. Wherever he went, fans of the opposing team loved to hate him. However, booing didn't bother him. In fact, it inspired him. But that didn't stop the rooters of the St. Louis Hawks, who were battling the San Francisco Warriors in the 1967 Western Division play-offs.

The Warriors won the first two games at home but lost the next two at Keil Auditorium in St. Louis. During the fourth game, Barry sprained his ankle. As he limped off the court, the unsympathetic St. Louis fans stood and gave him a derisive "boovation."

"That really upset me because I was hurt," Barry recalled. "I decided to say something about the fans' behavior and I didn't care what anyone thought."

Back in San Francisco, before the fifth game, Barry went on his regular five-minute radio show and blasted the fans' behavior. "St. Louis has the baseball Cardinals, the football Cardinals, and the basketball Hawks," Barry told his listeners. "St. Louis is really a town for the birds."

The St. Louis media picked up Barry's acid comments and by the time the series moved back to St. Louis for the sixth game (with the Warriors leading three games to two), the fans there were prepared to bury Barry—in garbage.

The Warriors were warned that a hostile reception awaited them. Team owner Franklin Mieuli hired a squad of rent-a-cops to stand behind the San Francisco bench and watch the Warriors' rear— especially Barry's. Coach Bill Sharman was so worried that the San Francisco dressing room was bugged or would be sabotaged that he had his players suit up in the hotel before going to the auditorium.

"The fans got on me right away," recalled Barry. "Snickers candy bars was the sponsor of my radio show, and when I was introduced before the game, the boos started and the Snickers bars came flying out of the stands. It was like a hail storm. Even some of their own players got hit."

The candy attack was just the beginning. Eggs, tomatoes, beer, and hot dogs (in honor of Barry's reputation around the league) continued to rain down on the court throughout the game. While players on both teams were forced to dodge salvos of food, officials halted play five times so maintenance crews could mop the mess of scrambled eggs and tomato paste off the court.

The bombardment did nothing to deter Barry. He rallied the Warriors from an 18-point deficit by blistering the nets for 41 points and snaring 11 rebounds.

With less than three minutes left in the game, and St. Louis ahead by two points, the partisan crowd definitely wanted something bad to happen to Barry. They got their wish—sort of. While leaping for a rebound in a crowd under the basket, Barry felt a sudden chill. That's when he discovered his shorts had been accidentally torn and ripped off.

The embarrassed star ran to the bench, wrapped a towel around his waist, and dashed through the howling crowd to the locker room. Barry donned a new pair of trunks and returned in time to take his revenge by hitting a pair of free throws and a field goal in the final minute of play to help seal the Warriors' 112–107 win that vaulted them into the finals.

Exposing himself to ridicule was nothing new for Barry. As a freshman for the University of Miami Hurricanes, Barry dove for a loose ball and felt the seams in the seat of his shorts give way.

The sight of the youngster spread-eagled on the floor with his rear end showing sent the crowd into hysterics. Barry rolled over and sat fixed to the floor until a trainer arrived with a face-saving towel. Barry wrapped himself in the towel and dashed off the court to peals of laughter. "It was," said Barry, "my most embarrassing moment—until it happened again in St. Louis."

KNOWING YOUR PLACE

During a 1982 Oral Roberts University practice, Assistant Coach Mike O'Rourke spotted benchwarmer Gerald Johnson taking shots from midcourt.

The coach told Johnson to quit fooling around and to shoot only from game-situation positions.

So Johnson did just that. He walked over to the bench, sat down, and took a shot from his seat.

FENNIS DEMBO

Forward ○ University of Wyoming Cowboys ○ December, 1987

Fennis Dembo—"Fennis the Menace" to his opponents—proved he was an all-America hot dog during a wild month of showboating on the court.

When the 6-foot, 5-inch forward played at Wyoming, part of his game was taunting opponents and their fans. "He loved to go on the

AP/Wide World Photos

road where he could get into it with the crowds," said Kevin McKinney, Wyoming's sports information director. "Whenever he scored, he'd turn to the fans and shake his fists in the air and urge them to boo louder—which they always did."

But Dembo outdid himself throughout December, 1987.

During a 100–68 blowout over the Colorado Buffaloes, Dembo deliberately incited the Colorado crowd to a fever pitch. "Each time Wyoming made a basket, he ran around the court yelling out the score and laughing and pointing at the scoreboard," recalled David Plati, Colorado's sports information director.

But what really sent the Buffaloes' fans and players into an uproar was Dembo's attempt to high-five his opponents. "He scored a basket and then came running in front of our bench giggling like a fool," said

Plati. "Then he tried to high-five [Colorado coach] Tom Miller. But when the coach ignored him, Dembo tried to get the guys on our team to give him five. They didn't, even though he tried that high-five crap more than once.

"Finally, they had enough of Mr. Hot Dog. So the next time he came around for his high five, they all stood up in unison and gave him the high *one*." Getting the bird didn't faze Dembo in the least.

A few weeks later, Wyoming, then ranked fifth in the nation, played at Boise State and barely squeaked by with a 59–55 victory. Despite the tight game, Dembo continued to play to the crowd all night long.

The score was tied late in the contest when Dembo went to the foul line to shoot a free throw. "It was a critical time in the game—a made-to-order situation for our fans," recalled Max Corbet, Boise State's sports information director. "They really started heaping him with abuse—and Dembo loved it.

"Before the referee gave him the ball, Dembo turned all the way around with his arms outstretched, waving his hands up and down like he was telling the crowd to give him more. Of course, that got them going even more."

Dembo basked in the magnitude of their antagonism and smiled. Then he stepped to the line for his free throw attempt, aimed . . . and missed.

"The noise was so loud you'd have thought the roof had caved in," said Corbet. "But it didn't bother him a bit. We rebounded the miss and while we were going down court, Dembo paused at the free throw line and did one of those four-corner bows to the crowd like you see boxers do in the Olympics. Miss or make, it didn't matter to Dembo. He was just happy showboating for the crowd."

Dembo's mouth was as inflammatory as his showboating. Before his team took off on a road trip to the University of Texas–El Paso and Brigham Young University, he told reporters: "We've got to go down there and sweep both of them. We're going to do it and you can put it in your newspapers so that they can read it." UTEP and BYU read Dembo's remarks—and then made him eat his words. Wyoming lost both games.

Cowboys coach Benny Dees tried to downplay Dembo's antics. But Dees eventually gave up. Following Wyoming's 1986 victory over Clemson, which put the Cowboys in the National Invitational Tournament, Dembo climbed the backboard, sat on the rim, and led the fans in cheers.

Dees watched him and told reporters, "Fennis has a great personality and is just a fine person." Then the coach paused and added, "Ah, let's face it. He's a hot dog."

HORACE "BONES" MCKINNEY

Forward ○ Washington Capitols–Boston Celtics ○ 1946–52

Bones McKinney was the Dizzy Dean of basketball.

He was an oversized clown, an emotional rogue, a superstitious wag. He played with the heart of an all-star and the soul of a Globetrotter.

Even before he made it to the pros, Bones began making a name for himself as a court jester. In 1946, when he helped lead the North Carolina Tar Heels to the NCAA championship finals, he gained a reputation for ribbing the refs. Sometimes when he was called for a foul, McKinney draped an arm around the official and said, "Don't mind that booing—we all make mistakes." Fans laughed when, after making a shot, Bones checked with the scorekeeper to make sure that he was given credit for the basket. He also gave pep talks to himself as he raced down the court.

From the moment he first stepped foot on the court as a Washington Capitol, fans knew he was slightly off center. Once, with two minutes left in a blowout over the New York Knicks, Bones was fouled. Rather than attempt a routine free throw, McKinney saw this as an opportunity for his unique brand of humor. He looked over at the Capitols' coach, Red Auerbach, and winked. Then he turned around and tossed the ball backward over his head. Unfortunately, he missed.

He always wanted to make the game fun—but sometimes his tomfoolery backfired. Once during a 1950 road trip, when Bones was the player-coach of the Capitols, he bumped into referee Chuck Solodare, who was registering at the same hotel as the team. The fun-loving McKinney suggested to the good-natured Solodare that they enliven an upcoming game with a little horseplay.

"Sure," said the ref. "We'll have to get together and give the fans a little show sometime."

The next night, Solodare was officiating a game between the St. Louis Bombers and the Capitols when he called a personal on McKinney. Bones, remembering the conversation from the day before, graciously salaamed Solodare. To the player's shock, the ref slapped Bones with a technical.

"Chuck! Chuck!" McKinney protested in a whisper. "The act, the act, remember?"

"The act?" said Solodare. *"I'll* tell you when the curtain goes up."

Even when McKinney got angry—which was seldom—he still managed to make people laugh. Once when Washington was battling the Bombers, Bones got ticked off at the St. Louis Arena organist, who was playing a loud funeral dirge every time a Capitols player stepped to the foul line. After each miss, the organist played a chord that sounded like a Bronx cheer, to the delight of the fans. Finally McKinney had heard enough. The next time he was fouled, he called time-out, strode calmly off the court, lifted the organist from his stool, and dumped him 20 feet away. Bones waved a finger in his face and admonished him to sit quietly. Then McKinney returned to the foul line, bowed low to the crowd, and sank the shot.

Bones was most animated when guarding Philadelphia's future Hall of Famer Joe Fulks, who he always complained "gets all the breaks from officials." Whenever McKinney was called for a foul on Fulks that Bones didn't think he deserved, he dropped to his knees and pounded the floor while yelling "No! No!" One time, he was even more dramatic. As Fulks stepped to the charity stripe after a foul on Bones, McKinney went into a deep salaam. When referee Pat Kennedy ordered Bones to "cut out the nonsense," Bones looked hurt. "In the pros," he told the ref, "you have to salaam to King Fulks." That cost him a technical.

McKinney often played in his own little world. During a 1947 game against the Detroit Falcons in Washington, Bones was pushed out of bounds and crashed into a row of temporary seats that flew in all directions. While Bones untangled himself, he didn't realize that play had continued at the other end of the court. McKinney nonchalantly got up and started dutifully shoving the strewn chairs off the playing surface. Washington fans screamed at Bones to get back in the game. Luckily, he woke up just as teammate Fred Scolari stole the ball at the other end. Scolari heaved a long pass to McKinney, who promptly laid it in for an easy basket.

Bones was just as superstitious as he was clownish. When the Capitols went on a 17-game winning streak in 1947, he tried to do everything exactly the same every day. He insisted on eating the same food, wearing the same clothes, and occupying the same place on the bench before the game. He even commanded his teammates to file in and out of the locker room in the same order. Wrote Shirley Povich in

The Washington Post, "He made it a point throughout the streak to visit the same people as on the day of the Caps' last victory. And it was thus that Bob Wolf, Washington radio sportscaster, was able to track McKinney down for an interview one day. At two o'clock, Wolf knew that Bones would stop by the same used-car lot he had been frequenting at exactly that hour for two weeks. Sure enough, Bones was there."

McKinney later admitted that his superstition was driving his wife nuts. "She was washing those same orange-colored socks that I wore every day for the three weeks we were on that 17-game win streak. She was also making me the same kind of soft-scrambled eggs every day."

McKinney's teammates put up with his superstitious quirks. In fact, they were entertained by them. Early in the winning streak, a fan sent McKinney a bare-bellied Oriental doll for good luck. Bones named it "Yehudi" and made it part of the Capitols' pregame routine. For several weeks, Bones' teammates complied with his wish that they kiss Yehudi on the belly before every game. The ritual ended when the Caps finally lost. After the game, McKinney tossed Yehudi into the crowd. So much for a good luck charm.

CRUD DUDS

• Wayne "Goose" Embry, now the general manager of the Cleveland Cavaliers, wound up wearing an opponent's uniform in his first game as an NBA player. When the Cincinnati Royals arrived in Minneapolis to play the Lakers in 1958, the rookie discovered that in his excitement he had left his gym bag in a friend's car parked at the Cincinnati airport. Embry still made his debut—but in a borrowed Lakers uniform turned inside out.

• Ohio University freshman Dick Garrison was red all over. After riding the bench for most of the 1953 season, Garrison was surprised when the coach ordered him into the game. Leaping to his feet, Garrison ripped off his warm-up jacket, peeled off his sweat pants— and then dashed madly for the safety of the locker room. There, Garrison donned the pair of trunks that he had forgotten to put on when he first suited up. He returned to the court, fully dressed but totally mortified.

• During the 1985–86 season, New Jersey Nets forward Otis Birdsong frequently complained about not getting enough playing time. But on a trip to New York to play the Knicks, Birdsong's lack of playing time was his own fault. He forgot to take along his uniform. By the time someone retrieved it, the first quarter was over. Meanwhile, Birdsong cooled his heels in the trainer's room watching the game on TV.

• Members of the Houston Rockets had a hard time telling if Seattle SuperSonics guard Avery Johnson was coming or going during a 1989 game. Johnson began the contest with his playing shorts on backward. He finally rotated the shorts during a time-out while his teammates huddled around him.

• During a critical time-out late in a 1988 game against Texas A&M, Rice coach Scott Thompson flung his clipboard to the floor to emphasize a point. Suddenly, he felt a draft from behind.

To his chagrin, the coach discovered that his overexertion had overextended the seams of his pants and the seat had ripped open—widely.

"All I could do was sit there with a dumb look on my face," Thompson recalled. "The kids thought I had had a stroke. I felt helpless glued to my seat so I eventually took off my suit coat and wrapped it around my waist. We needed a strong rebounder on the team. But what I really needed in that game was a handy tailor."

JERRY EAVES

Forward ○ Utah Jazz ○ Oct. 21, 1983

In the hairiest ordeal ever suffered by an NBA player, Jerry Eaves took himself out of a game—because his hair was falling out.

A few hours before the Utah Jazz were slated to play an exhibition game with the Phoenix Suns in Las Vegas, Eaves decided he needed a trim. He wanted to look sharp because after the game he planned on sampling the glitzy showbiz night life of the neon city.

But since there wasn't enough time before the game to find a barber, Eaves recruited teammate J. J. Anderson to do the clip job.

Anderson was better at cutting off the fast break than he was at cutting off a little hair. He took off a lot. In fact, when Anderson finished, Eaves looked like he had tangled with a buzz saw—and lost.

It was enough to make his hair stand on end; that is, where he had hair left.

"J. J. really chopped it up," recalled Eaves. "Some off here, none off there. It looked like hell."

What was even worse was the unsightly new bald spot that he now sported on the top of his head. Eaves was beside himself with grief. In fact, he was so desperate that he grabbed a big clump of hair off the floor and glued it onto his head. He prayed that the patchwork job would hold up throughout the game.

However, toward the end of the second quarter, Eaves' sweat loosened his makeshift toupee. Then his worst fear was realized. "I went to the basket on one play and somebody really clobbered me on the head," said Eaves. "The chunk of hair fell off right out there in front of all those people.

"There were only a couple of minutes left to play in the half. I couldn't stand it. I imagined that all the rest of my hair would fall off too, so I ran off the court and yelled at [Utah coach] Frank Layden that I had to go."

The unflappable Jazz coach shrugged as his partially scalped power forward dashed out the door with his hair in his hand. Eaves then hailed a cab outside Thomas Mack Arena and ordered the driver to take him to the nearest barber.

"But there weren't any barbershops open at night," Eaves recalled. "And there I was, all sweaty, still in uniform, flying through the middle of Las Vegas, yelling at that poor driver to hurry up because I only had 15 minutes before the second half started."

Meanwhile, back at the arena, the Jazz couldn't find hide nor hair—especially hair—of Eaves. But just before the second half began, Eaves showed up. Since he had failed to locate a barber, the player was more desperate than ever. There was only one thing left to do. Eaves ordered Anderson to shave off the rest of his hair.

Eaves then returned to the game—bald but beautiful.

"Oh, man," moaned Eaves. "I was so embarrassed. J. J. thought it was hilarious. After it grew back out, nobody except my own personal barber ever touched my hair again."

HOT ROD HUNDLEY

Guard ○ Los Angeles Lakers ○ 1957–63

The way Hot Rod Hundley played, he should have been called Hot Dog. That's because he was one.

Hundley starred for the University of West Virginia Mountaineers and then the Los Angeles Lakers. He missed his calling by not playing on the only team that truly fit his style—the Harlem Globetrotters.

Hot Rod was just as happy to score some laughs as he was points. As a freshman at West Virginia in 1954, Hundley spiced up boring blowouts by taking shots from behind his back, spinning the ball on his fingertips, mugging it up for fans, hanging from baskets, and joking with the officials.

Incredibly, in one six-game stretch, he didn't even take a shot because the competition was too easy. Instead, he put on a "floor show" during the game. In fact, he was so entertaining that sometimes the freshman team outdrew the varsity in attendance.

When he made the varsity squad, Hot Rod continued his on-court antics. In a game against George Washington University, Hundley went to the line for two free throws. He made a hook shot from the foul line and then tossed in the second shot from behind his back.

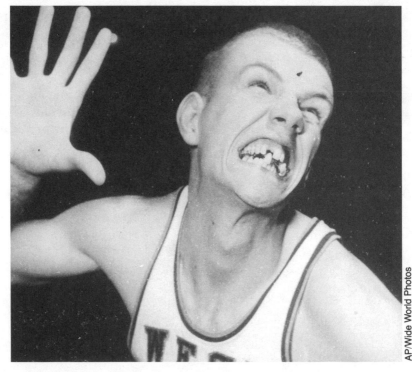

Against the University of Richmond, the Mountaineers had a six-point lead with 1:30 left. Hundley killed the remaining time by dribbling circles around the other team and rolling the ball up his arm, over his shoulders, and down the other arm whenever an opponent lunged for it. When the clock ran down to three seconds, Hot Rod tossed the ball high into the arena's rafters so that it hit the floor as time expired.

Hundley invented a zany shot that never failed to send fans into a wild frenzy. He would kneel on the floor about ten feet from the basket and attempt a one-handed set shot. More often than not, he made the wacky basket.

Even when Hot Rod had a cold spell, he still triggered laughs. Once after missing five straight shots in a game, Hot Rod chinned up the basket support and looked down the net to make sure there was nothing obstructing it.

Whenever Coach Fred Schaus took him out of the game for more than a few minutes, Hundley would stand on the bench, turn to the fans in the stands, and lead a roaring chant of "We want Hundley! We want Hundley!" Usually, he would be back on the court within seconds.

As the most publicized player to graduate in 1957, Hot Rod wound up with the Lakers. Although he never matched his college stats as a pro, his style made him a crowd favorite.

During a Lakers game, he spotted singer-actress Doris Day in a front row seat. He dribbled over to her and told the star that his next shot was for her. When he badly missed a hook shot, Hundley apologized as he ran past her and added, "But I tried, baby. I tried."

Hundley never let the exhausting NBA schedule interfere with his love for the night life. He once said that he "slept all day and went out all night and squeezed the ball games in-between."

Whenever the team played in New York, said former Laker Tom Hawkins, "Hundley would phone a teammate's hotel room and say in a dramatic voice, 'It's now six o'clock. The streets of the naked city beckon us.' Then he would tell about all the glorious things in store for the evening. For him, nothing was more disastrous than an overtime game in New York. It cut into his social life."

Although he was more style than substance on the court, Hot Rod was fond of regaling fans with what he called one of his "greatest performances." Said Hundley, "That was the game in which Elgin Baylor and I combined for 78 points." Hot Rod sometimes failed to mention that Elgin scored 71 of those points.

HACK ATTACK

With the way they hack opponents, it's a good thing the hatchetmen of basketball aren't lumberjacks or we wouldn't have any forests left. These guys get more whistles than Madonna. They charge more often than a hopeless shopaholic. Their more serious infractions can turn the game into a basketbrawl. For "The Most Outrageous Fouls," The Basketball Hall of SHAME inducts the following:

BILL LAIMBEER

Center ○ Detroit Pistons ○ June 10, 1990

Bill Laimbeer once tried to foul an opposing player *before* the game even started. But he wound up bowling over an unsuspecting photographer instead.

The pregame charging foul by the Detroit Pistons' baddest Bad Boy merely enhanced his reputation as the NBA's ultimate hatchet man. Around the league, Laimbeer has been called the Ax Murderer, the Prince of Darkness, the Consummate Provocateur, and His Heinous.

The 6-foot, 11-inch, 245-pound center tried to live up to those sobriquets when the Pistons were taking the floor in game three of the 1990 NBA finals with the Portland Trail Blazers.

According to Detroit tradition, Laimbeer leads the Pistons onto the court in their pregame lay-up line and tries to smash-dunk the first shot with enough force to send the needle flying off the Richter scale.

But as he approached the floor at Portland's Memorial Coliseum, Laimbeer saw that some Blazers were about to beat him to the court and steal his thunder. So Laimbeer grabbed a ball and roared straight for the Blazers' 6-foot, 3-inch guard Terry Porter.

"I was going to knock Porter on his ass, but he got away," recalled

Kirthmon Dozier/*The Detroit News*

Laimbeer. "So I aimed for [center] Wayne Cooper, but he saw me coming and ducked aside."

After the two Blazers gave him the slip, the only one in Laimbeer's path was Michael Lloyd, a 5-foot, 9-inch, 160-pound photographer for *The Portland Oregonian,* whose back was turned. Lloyd and several other lensmen were on the floor to snap pictures of the Blazers' entrance onto the court. But before he could take a photo, Lloyd was sent sprawling when Laimbeer creamed him.

"I was waiting for the players to come out and the next thing I knew I was sliding across the court," recalled Lloyd. "When I came to my senses, I was staring straight up under the Pistons' basket. [Forward] Dennis Rodman was jumping back and forth over me, laughing and pointing at Laimbeer.

"Laimbeer was out to blast somebody, so he blindsided me. I never saw him coming. Other people had to tell me the name of the steamroller that flattened me—including my doctor and my attorney, who were in the stands. The lawyer urged me to 'sue the bastard.' He said he'd love to get Laimbeer in front of a local judge and jury." But Lloyd, who fortunately was not hurt, chose to drop the matter.

Steve Nehl, another photographer on the floor who witnessed the Laimbeer stampede, added, "There's no doubt in anybody's mind who saw it that Laimbeer deliberately went after Michael just because he missed a crack at one of the Blazers.

"Michael went skidding on his back. The Pistons just kept trucking right on by him, laughing and grinning as though Laimbeer did this all the time. It was no big deal to them."

Laimbeer never bothered to apologize. "If I'm going to get in a collision, the other guy is going to get the worst of it," said Laimbeer. "The photographer was in the way. I had to run over him."

Phoenix Suns forward Kurt Rambis, who still carries the marks of bruises from big Bill, wasn't surprised after learning of the "foul" by the player everyone loves to hate. "I assume his parents like him," said Rambis. "But you'd have to verify that."

Joked Laimbeer's teammate, Isiah Thomas, "Bill is really a good-hearted person. It's just that he has no conscience."

JUNGLE JIM LOSCUTOFF

Forward ○ Boston Celtics ○ Nov. 15, 1956

Jim Loscutoff committed the most embarrassing foul in NBA history. He was caught holding George Yardley's shorts—when Yardley was no longer in them!

Although Jungle Jim was known throughout his career as one of the Boston Celtics' most intimidating hatchet men, his favorite tactic was a sneak attack from the rear. He liked to grab and hold his opponent by the seat of the shorts.

Loscutoff was so deft at this sly bit of defensive chicanery that he usually got away with it. But there was one time when Loscutoff was left holding the bag—or rather the baggy shorts.

During a 1956 preseason game in Boston, the Ft. Wayne Pistons were lined up at the free throw line for an in-bounds play underneath the basket. Knowing that Yardley, Ft. Wayne's agile forward, would likely break behind a double screen, Loscutoff crowded close behind his man and got a good grip on the back of Yardley's shorts.

Basketball Hall of Fame

"When they threw the ball in, George jumped and the shorts just ripped right off him," recalled Loscutoff. "I was standing there holding his pants, he was standing there in just his jock, and both of us were standing there with our mouths open.

"For a couple of seconds everything just froze. The rest of the players were as surprised as we were. Then George ran around in a couple of circles screaming his head off. He got to the bench, found a towel to cover up with, and dashed off to the locker room while the crowd howled."

Loscutoff tossed the tattered drawers toward the Ft. Wayne bench, while the referee, who nearly swallowed his whistle making the call, signaled the holding foul against the Celtic.

"I'm not sure who was more embarrassed—me for getting caught holding, or George for getting caught with his pants down," said Jungle Jim. "At least George hid out in the locker room. I had to stand out there in the middle of the floor holding his drawers with nowhere to go.

"The crowd sure loved it, even if it was a foul against one of their guys."

Asked about the ignoble foul, Yardley grudgingly admitted, "Jim claims that I ran off the floor in shame. That's the de-panter's story. But I had nothing to hide. I calmly walked off the court and got a new pair of shorts. And that's straight from the de-pantee."

Loscutoff's teammate, center Bill Russell, recalled the naked foul with glee this way: "It was the easiest holding call any ref has ever had to make."

CONNIE DIERKING

Center ○ Syracuse Nationals ○ Nov. 15, 1959

When Connie Dierking finally got the chance to show his stuff, the towering rookie hacked down the Cincinnati Royals like a mad Paul Bunyan chopping his way through a forest.

In less than ten minutes of furious fouling, the 6-foot, 10-inch center collected his full quota of six personals and became the first player in NBA history to foul out of a game in the opening period.

"It was embarrassing fouling out that fast," admitted Dierking. He grew up in Cincinnati, starred at the University of Cincinnati, and dreamed of being drafted by the Cincinnati Royals. But he went to Syracuse in the first round and sat on the Nats' bench as backup to the team's star center, Johnny "Red" Kerr.

When Syracuse met Cincinnati during a doubleheader at the old Madison Square Garden, Dierking begged player-coach Paul Seymour for playing time to show the Royals what they had missed by not picking him. So Seymour put Dierking in early in the first quarter.

"I wanted to show them they'd made a big mistake, but it really backfired," recalled Dierking. "I fouled so fast that Coach Seymour didn't have a chance to get me out."

Dierking's foul spree began the instant he checked in—he promptly body-checked Wayne Embry, the Royals' hefty center, into the second row. Embry barely made it back onto the court before he was hammered again by Dierking.

Embry wasn't the only one who spent the next several minutes trying to avoid Dierking. Jack Twyman, the Royals' all-star forward, was another target. Four of Twyman's 38 game points came from free throws, courtesy of being hacked by the overeager rookie.

"I remember clobbering Wayne Embry pretty good a couple of times," said Dierking. "But after that, the fouls are a big blur. Before I knew it, I was back on the bench wondering what happened."

Coach Seymour said he had some misgivings about starting Dierking because of his penchant for fouling. "Connie was complaining about sitting on the bench," he recalled. "So when he started making a lot of noise about playing against Cincinnati, I decided to put him in and let him go. That took care of his bellyaching. He learned real quick why I kept him on the bench."

Said Dierking, "Fouling out in the first quarter was a dubious honor. And it was doubly frustrating and humiliating because it was against Cincinnati. Needless to say, it was not the proudest night of my career."

NEW YORK JETS AND NEW YORK GIANTS
March 22, 1989

The New York Jets and the New York Giants proved that when you mix football with basketball, you get basketbrawl.

The two intracity NFL rivals turned a charity hoops game into a bare-knuckles melee that brought out the cops.

Players from both teams had agreed to set aside their animosity toward each other in an effort to raise money for a good cause. Promising to put behind all the years of bad-mouthing and name-calling, members of the Jets and Giants showed up at Wagner College on Staten Island to play in the charity basketball event. At the time, the Giants were still smarting from being knocked out of play-off contention by the Jets in a 27–21 loss in the final game of the 1988 season.

Their basketball game was the second half of a double bill benefiting the Rocco Laurie Foundation, which provides scholarships for underprivileged kids.

"The first game was Cops versus Teachers," said Rich Vitaliano, chief of security for the small college. "As it turned out, we needed all the cops we could get during the second game."

The fussing and feuding started right after the tip-off—an elbow here, a knee there, a hard shove under the boards. The referees tried to curb the rough stuff by calling numerous fouls. But by the end of the first half, any resemblance to a civilized charity game had disappeared and the Wagner gym began to look more like a ring for Wrestlemania.

"We could see what was coming," Vitaliano said. "The Jets and Giants had played here before and their games usually got ugly, but this was the worst. The referees wanted to call it off at halftime, but we talked to the guys and they promised to behave.

"We tried speeding up the game in the second half by not stopping the clock on fouls or time-outs, just so we could get the thing over with before there was a lot of damage. But [Giants tight end] Zeke Mowatt caught me at it and yelled that if I didn't run the clock right, he'd take over."

As the pushing turned to punching, the fans—evenly divided between Jets and Giants supporters—started booing both sides and tossing paper cups at the combatants.

"It was really getting out of hand," Vitaliano said. "Just about that time, [Jets tight end] Keith Neubert and [Giants running back] George Adams started punching. Then Neubert and [Giants defensive back] Sheldon White went at it. That cleared the benches and everybody jumped in. I tried to break it up, but it was unbelievable trying to get in between those monsters when they were that mad."

Other cops attending the game poured onto the floor to help Vitaliano. The basketbrawlers were finally separated and Vitaliano ordered the game suspended with three minutes still on the clock and the Giants leading 91–75.

"I think most of them wanted somebody to stop it," Vitaliano said. "There were lots of bruises and black eyes. It wasn't a wrestling match like you usually see in NBA fights. They were throwing real haymakers out there."

Rich Kottie, the Jets' offensive coordinator at the time and a Wagner College alumnus, had helped organize the charity game. He was also doing the color commentary for a Staten Island cable company that was televising the contest live when the fist swinging broke out in front of his table.

"It was pretty embarrassing," Kottie recalled. "I brought those guys in there to help raise money. All they did was raise hell with each other.

"A lot of them were surprised when the punches started flying.

They forgot they didn't have the usual helmets and pads on to protect them. Getting punched without a face mask hurts. Served them right."

GIVING HIM THE FINGER

During a 1953 game, Minneapolis Lakers star George Mikan dislocated his finger while committing a foul.

Mikan, who was having a rare off night, went to the bench, where Lakers coach John Kundla tried yanking the finger back into position while chewing out the player.

Mikan kept trying to interrupt, but Kundla silenced him each time with "Shut up and listen to me!"

Finally, Mikan managed to break in long enough to say, "Okay, Coach, but all I wanted to tell you was that you're pulling the wrong finger."

DAVE COWENS

Center ○ Boston Celtics ○ Jan. 26, 1973

Dave Cowens demonstrated the difference between a real foul and a fake one—much to the pain of Houston Rocket Mike Newlin.

During his ten-year career with the Boston Celtics, the hard-nosed, emotional center became a legend for racking up personal fouls. Cowens, who led the league in fouls two years in a row, admitted he deserved most of the calls for the way he aggressively defended his turf at the high post.

But he hated being whistled on the close calls—and absolutely despised players on defense who would fake being the victim of a charge to draw an offensive foul. Cowens believed it was immoral to fall down unless one was truly knocked down.

Cowens showed just how much he disapproved of the fake flops when the Houston Rockets played in Boston in 1973.

With the Celtics on offense, Cowens set a pick at the post, then turned to face the basket, and nudged Calvin Murphy, the Rockets' 5-foot, 9-inch spark-plug guard. In an Oscar-winning performance, Murphy went sprawling and, as the Rocket had hoped, the ref whistled Cowens for the charging foul. The Celtics' center vigorously argued the call, but the ball still went over to Houston.

Basketball Weekly

Minutes later, it happened again. This time, the Rockets' other guard, Mike Newlin, in another fine acting job, toppled to the floor and drew the offensive foul call against the now smoldering Cowens.

On the bench, Boston coach Red Auerbach knew Cowens' normally short fuse was burning. "Dave was a scrapper," recalled Auerbach. "This foolishness was eating him up. I knew something was going to happen when I saw the fire come into his eyes."

Newlin didn't see the fire, but he soon felt the explosion. "There's absolutely nothing a player hates any worse than getting called for an offensive foul, and Dave had just been called for two in a row," recalled Newlin.

"We got the ball out of bounds. I took the inbounds pass and went sprinting downcourt on a semi-fast break since we outnumbered Boston with Cowens still in the back court bitching over the call.

"All of a sudden Dave realized what was happening and came racing across the court. He smashed into me with both forearms like he was playing linebacker in the NFL and sent me flying. I didn't even see him coming. Cowens was just pissed off over the call and I was the first guy he saw in a Houston uniform. He really nailed me from behind."

The blow deposited Newlin several rows up in the courtside seats. But even before the stunned Rocket came to rest, Cowens turned to referee Bill Jones and screamed for all the Garden to hear: "Now *that's* a foul!"

OTIS SMITH

Guard ○ Jacksonville University Dolphins ○ March 2, 1984

When Otis Smith fouled out for the first time in his collegiate career, he didn't quite know what to do. So he simply stayed in the game— until he was caught.

As a result, Smith was disqualified twice in the same game!

The Jacksonville University Dolphins' guard was playing a gritty, aggressive game against the Old Dominion University Monarchs. But then he was whistled for his fifth foul with 2:44 left to play and the Monarchs ahead by three points, 65–62. Before the ODU player could shoot the free throws resulting from Smith's foul, a time-out was called and both teams huddled up at their benches.

Meanwhile, referee Joe Forte notified the scorer's table that the Dolphins' star was out of the game. But Smith and JU coach Bob Wenzel claimed they never got the message.

When play resumed, Smith strolled back onto the court and continued playing for the next minute and a half. Unfortunately, Smith blew his cover when he sank a basket with 1:08 remaining.

It took another eight seconds before it dawned on Forte that Smith belonged on the bench, not on the floor scoring points. Although he let the basket count, the ref whistled a technical against JU for using a fouled-out player. Coach Wenzel vigorously protested the call, arguing that he hadn't been told about Smith's earlier DQ.

But the protest fell on deaf ears and Smith was disqualified for the second time in the game.

His failure to sit down on the bench took the steam out of any momentum the Dolphins had hoped to build down the stretch. The Monarchs made both free throws off the technical, got the ball out of bounds, and immediately scored again. Then they coasted to an 11-point victory, 79–68, and eliminated the Dolphins in the first round of the 1984 Sun Coast Conference tournament finals.

"I don't think it was fair that they hit us with a technical," griped Wenzel after the game. "Besides, Otis had an excuse. That was the only time all year he fouled out. He just wasn't used to sitting on the bench."

GUY RODGERS   JIM LOSCUTOFF

Guard ○ Philadelphia Warriors   **Forward ○ Boston Celtics**

Nov. 25, 1959

In a brawl that had the crowd holding their sides from laughter, Guy Rodgers and Jungle Jim Loscutoff tangled in a one-punch fight that was more slapstick than slapface.

The 6-foot Rodgers, weighing in at 185 pounds, showed either great courage or great stupidity when he rabbit-punched the hulking 6-foot, 5-inch, 230-pound Loscutoff, one of the most feared foulers in the NBA.

But the little Warrior at least had enough sense to take off after he threw the sneaky haymaker, because the enraged Celtic was bellowing for his hide.

During the 1959 game, which was being played in the Boston Garden, Philadelphia's Wilt Chamberlain and Boston's Sam Jones got into a shoving match under the basket.

"Sam picked up one of the chairs the ball boys sat on," recalled Loscutoff. "He warned Wilt that if he took another step he'd bop him over the head with the stool.

"Nobody else was involved in the argument. We were just standing around in the middle of the court watching. For some reason, Guy walked up behind me and punched me in the back of the head. I guess he figured that if there was going to be a riot he wanted to get his licks in early and get out before the rest of us got started."

Stunned by the unexpected punch, Loscutoff whirled around and glared down at Rodgers. "Why'd you do that, you little SOB?" demanded the menacing Loscutoff.

Rodgers blanched and, recognizing his foolish error in judgment, looked around for a quick escape. He spun on his heels and took off with Loscutoff in hot pursuit.

Rodgers ran down one sideline, around behind the basket, and up the other side of the court. Right behind him came the lumbering Loscutoff, braying for Rodgers' scalp. Fortunately for Rodgers, he was a better track man than a boxer and was able to outdistance his pursuer.

"I chased him around and around the court," recalled Loscutoff. "He finally jumped over his own bench and ran up into the crowd. When I went after him, all his teammates grabbed me and held me so Guy could escape to the locker room. He stayed hidden down there and they brought in a substitute—somebody who wouldn't run away."

Referee Richie Powers said the Rodgers-Loscutoff brouhaha looked more like a Keystone Kops chase scene than an NBA fight.

"Picture this," Powers recalled. "There we were in the center of the court watching the great chase, doubled over with laughter. For some reason, Loscutoff never tried to head Rodgers off on the court. The two players simply ran around the perimeter of the court, until Rodgers spun toward an exit and galloped to the Philadelphia dressing room.

"I don't want to think what would have happened if Jungle Jim had caught Rodgers that night."

JACK LOOMIS

Center ○ Stanford University Cardinal ○ Jan. 29, 1972

In the time it takes for most players to warm up and get into the flow of the game, Jack Loomis was whistled to the bench.

He set the (sub)standard for quick foul-outs. Incredibly, Loomis averaged a foul every 46 seconds of playing time!

Loomis, a 6-foot, 10-inch transfer student from Harvard, achieved overnight infamy after spending most of the season languishing on the bench as a reserve for Stanford. He was sent into a 1972 game against Air Force with about five minutes to go in the first half—and didn't even make it to halftime.

Eager to be noticed in front of the Stanford crowd, Loomis played defense with the finesse of a pit bull. He tried to bully every player in an Air Force uniform. He mugged them. He clubbed them. He hacked them. And he was caught every time.

In just over three minutes, Loomis collected four defensive fouls. And moments later, after playing only three minutes and 50 seconds, he was whistled out of the game after collecting his fifth personal.

The last foul was the most embarrassing of all his infractions. Loomis was called for an offensive foul after he charged down the lane—and missed an easy lay-up while plowing into a defender.

Holding his head in disbelief at such a quick DQ, the fouling flash trudged to the bench, hoping to disappear among the other bench-warmers. But the Stanford fans—recognizing Loomis' feat as an historic moment—weren't about to let him hide quietly. They gave Loomis a standing ovation. And at halftime, spectators crowded around the abashed basher seeking his autograph, which he reluctantly signed.

SHOOTING MOST FOUL

It goes by two names: free throw, which it almost is when someone like Larry Bird is at the line; and foul shot, which it certainly is when a "bricklayer" goes to the charity stripe. The foul foul shooters bang it off the glass, clang it off the rim, or hang up an air ball. The only things they sink are the stomachs of their teammates. For "The Most Inept Free Throw Shooting," The Basketball Hall of SHAME inducts the following:

CHRIS DUDLEY

Center ○ New Jersey Nets ○ April 14, 1990

In the worst free throw shooting performance in NBA history, Chris Dudley went to the line 18 times in one game—and missed the hoop every time but once!

The New Jersey Nets' 6-foot, 11-inch center put up more bricks than a mason working on a skyscraper. Thanks to his horrendous 1-for-18 foul shooting, the Nets lost 124–113 to the visiting Indiana Pacers.

In the fourth quarter, when the Nets were trying to make a run, Dudley missed his last 13 foul shots in a row. No NBA player had ever missed the mark that badly—although Hall of Famer Wilt Chamberlain had come close 30 years earlier when he clunked ten straight foul shots in a game.

During Dudley's 0-for-13 string, he rattled the backboard with five booming bricks and once missed everything with an air ball. As Dudley continued to shoot his free throws everywhere but in the basket, the 9,235 Nets fans in the Byrne Meadowlands Arena sensed history in the making.

Every time Dudley got the ball in the fourth quarter, the fans yelled at the Pacers, "Foul him! Foul him!" Whenever he was fouled, the crowd cheered. And every time he missed, the fans cheered even louder and chanted, "Dudley! Dudley!" For reasons known only to them, the fans kept waving dollar bills at him.

Dudley's desperate attempts to sink just one free throw became so pitiful that referee Dick Bavetta actually felt sorry for him. Before one of Dudley's free throw attempts, Bavetta handed Dudley the ball, patted him on the back, and encouraged him to make the shot. Dudley missed.

Another time, teammate Chris Moore clasped his hands in prayer as Dudley stepped to the line. Once, the Nets' Purvis Short tried to sneak to the foul line after Dudley was fouled but Bavetta caught him.

Looking on the bright side, New Jersey coach Bill Fitch, whose team was trailing by 23 points in the fourth quarter, claimed that Dudley's dismal performance was actually an inspiration. "I'm sitting there and it's like a morgue in the arena," said Fitch. "It's like I'm at a funeral. But his missed free throws ignited the fans and helped us start a rally."

But the rally fell short, mainly because the Pacers deliberately fouled Dudley every time he handled the ball in the closing minutes. Indiana committed 36 fouls in the game, 15 more than the Nets.

"You didn't have to be a rocket scientist to know they were going to foul me every time I got my hands on the ball," said Dudley, who wound up with a league-low free throw shooting percentage of .342 for the season.

"That's the worst I've ever done in a game," admitted the foul foul shooter. "I'd shoot one and it would come up short. The next time I'd think about it too much and I would bang it off the back of the rim."

Dudley's shooting that night was even more awful than that of a blindfolded fan. As part of a Nets halftime promotion, a fan was picked from the stands, blindfolded, spun around three times, and handed the ball at the foul line. He made one out of seven free throws.

Dudley's reputation as a dud at the charity stripe had been sealed the previous season when he played for the Cleveland Cavaliers. On January 29, 1989, in a 122–117 loss to the Washington Bullets, Dudley missed five straight free throw attempts—on one trip to the foul line!

Dudley was fouled and had two shots coming. No one was surprised when he missed them both. But on the second try, Washington's Darrell Walker was whistled for being in the lane too soon.

So Dudley got a third shot. He missed. This time Bullets center Dave Feitl jumped too soon. So Dudley got a fourth shot. He missed. But referee Earl Strom called Feitl for being in the lane again. So

Dudley got a fifth shot. He missed. Dudley's performance was foul shooting at its foulest.

TOM BOERWINKLE

Center ○ Chicago Bulls ○ March 18, 1969

In the days of the penalty foul shot, missing three straight free throws was called a turkey. Tom Boerwinkle bagged his bird at the worst possible moment.

Chicago's rookie center had the chance to single-handedly beat the Los Angeles Lakers in the final seconds of a 1969 game and keep the Bulls' playoff hopes alive.

The Lakers were ahead by one point with two seconds left to play at the Chicago Stadium. Boerwinkle was fouled and went to the line in the penalty situation with three chances to make two shots.

"If Tom makes just one of the three, the game goes into overtime," recalled Chicago coach Dick Motta. "Two and we win. Miss all three and we can forget the play-offs.

"We forgot the play-offs."

With only four games left on the regular schedule, the Bulls were still in the hunt for a playoff spot. L.A. had already wrapped up the Western Division title. Before the game Motta told his bunch of young, inexperienced players that beating the powerful Lakers could give the Bulls the kind of boost they needed to win their remaining games and make the play-offs.

"Right down to the last couple of seconds, we thought we would win," recalled Boerwinkle. "And we might have if I hadn't choked."

Chicago erased a five-point Lakers lead in the final two minutes of the game. With only seconds remaining and the Bulls trailing 93–92, Boerwinkle tried to bang in a shot from ten feet out. But Lakers center Wilt Chamberlain blocked the shot. However, in the ensuing scramble, Boerwinkle got the ball back and threw up a last-second desperation shot.

He missed. But Boerwinkle was fouled by Jerry West. So, with two seconds left, Boerwinkle stepped to the line with the golden opportunity to be a hero in his first season in the NBA. Once, during his senior year at Tennessee, Boerwinkle was faced with a similar pressure-packed situation. He canned both free throws to win the game.

But this was different. This was the NBA.

The rookie, a 65 percent free throw shooter, took a deep breath and then tossed up his first shot. It hit the back of the rim, rattled around inside the net, and popped back out.

"I saw the blood drain out of Tom's face," recalled Motta. "He hadn't considered the possibility of missing all three until that first one. I didn't want to watch the second shot, so I turned around to get a drink. I heard the crowd groan and turned back just in time to see the ball fall short. I thought to myself, 'Oh, come on, Tom. Just make one.'"

Now the Bulls' entire season was down to one simple free throw. But the pressure was too much. Boerwinkle overcompensated and banged the ball hard off the backboard. The game was over. The Bulls had lost.

"I thought the first two free throws at least had a chance of going in," recalled Boerwinkle. "The third one was a total brick. I sure wish they had designated shooters. My God, that basket could have been 14 feet wide and I still wouldn't have made it.

"I blame Jerry West for that disaster," he added with tongue in cheek. "He was the one who fouled me and sent me to the line with a three-to-make-two. I wouldn't have blown the game if it hadn't been for West.

"Some guys go their entire careers without ever seeing a turkey. I had the misfortune of bagging my first turkey in my rookie year."

WILT CHAMBERLAIN

Center ○ Philadelphia/San Francisco Warriors–Philadelphia 76ers– Los Angeles Lakers ○ 1959–73

Wilt Chamberlain is the patron saint of free throw shooters most foul.

As great a player as he was—the 7-foot, 1-inch Hall of Famer is the NBA's all-time second-leading scorer—the Stilt wilted at the charity stripe. While most NBA stars shoot at least .700 from the line, Chamberlain barely reached .500.

In fact, Wilt missed more foul shots than any player in NBA history. He attempted 11,862 free throws and missed 5,805 for an embarrassing career mark of .511—and that's lower than his fine lifetime field goal percentage of .540!

Chamberlain outdid himself in the 1967–68 season. Of 932 free throw attempts, he clunked 578 for an atrocious .380 shooting average. It was one of six seasons in which he missed more free throws than he made.

"It's ridiculous," said Philadelphia 76ers coach Dolph Schayes in 1965. "Any high school kid could do better."

In 1961 Wilt scored 44 points against the Detroit Pistons—but went 0-for-10 from the charity stripe to set a record for most free throws attempted without making one. Second place in the record book is an 0-for-9 performance by—you guessed it—Wilt Chamberlain.

Over the years, everyone—except the opposing teams—offered solutions to solve Chamberlain's baffling charity case. Coaches and teammates gave him pointers. Thousands of fans sent in good luck charms, special prayers, and tips such as shoot backward, shoot with your eyes closed, shoot left-handed.

Wilt tried shooting free throws underhanded, overhead, one-handed, two-handed, side saddle, from the middle of the line, from the right side, from the left side.

Chamberlain despaired over ever finding a cure for his chronic bricklaying. In his autobiography, *Wilt,* he bemoaned his reputation as a foul foul shooter: "I got mad and embarrassed and tried everything I could think of to improve. But the harder I tried—the more different ways I tried to shoot—the worse I got.

"I'd try a new stance and a new grip and a new style every few games, but I never felt comfortable at the free throw line. . . . By my ninth year I was down to 38 percent."

One year the Warriors were so desperate to improve Wilt's free throw production that they hired Cy Kaselman, a star for Philadelphia in the 1920s. Kaselman, who one year shot a blistering .950 from the line, taught Wilt how to shoot free throws underhanded.

For a while it worked. Chamberlain's percentage rose at times to as high as 70 percent. "But," recalled Wilt, "I felt silly—like a sissy—shooting underhanded. I'd start out shooting that way some years, and then I'd get cocky and figure I could do just as well shooting one-handed. As soon as I did that my percentage would drop like it had an anchor tied to it."

Finally, when it became obvious his horrendous record would never improve, Chamberlain said he no longer felt "quite the paranoia and humiliation I once did on the line, with everyone laughing and booing and all."

Toward the end of his otherwise spectacular career, the superstar brushed aside his reputation as the foulest foul shooter ever. He simply declared, "They don't pay me to make free throws."

GARFIELD SMITH

Forward ○ Boston Celtics ○ Nov. 17, 1971

Nothing is more shameful for a free throw shooter than to toss up an air ball. Garfield Smith knows that better than anyone. During one pitiful trip to the foul line, Smith threw up not one, not two, but *three* air balls in a row!

Smith played only two years in the NBA, but he lasted long enough to leave his mark on the charity stripe—a skid mark.

In his rookie year with the Boston Celtics, the 6-foot, 9-inch forward from Eastern Kentucky University instantly became one of the league's worst free throw shooters. That first season in Boston, Smith managed to convert only 22 of 56 foul shots for a dismal .393 average.

The next year, Smith hit on only six of 31 from the line and his average nosedived to a deplorable .194, definitely making him the NBA's worst foul shooter. But at least most of his free throw attempts managed to hit iron.

Not until a 1971 game against the Phoenix Suns did Smith establish himself as the league's air ball champion.

Late in the Celtics' 140–121 romp over the Suns, Boston coach Tom Heinsohn let his bench play. Soon after Smith checked in, he was fouled and went to the line for a three-to-make-two bonus situation that applied at the time.

He missed all three chances—but at least he missed with style. Not one shot touched the rim, the backboard, or the net.

Smith's teammate Don Nelson was among those waiting for either a basket or a rebound when Smith's free throws found nothing but air. "We were all giggling," recalled Nelson. "Smith missed them all— one went way left, one went way right, and one was way short."

Recounting his foulest foul line moment, Smith begged to differ with Nelson's recollection.

"The last one wasn't way short like Don said," claimed Smith. "It was *way, way, way* short. I probably could have come closer if I'd sat the ball down and walked away.

"The Celtics—and Don Nelson especially—teased me a lot about the air ball hat trick, missing three in a row that way. They told me I should be playing hockey."

COURT JESTERS

They are the jokers of basketball. They love to pull off pranks as much as they do last-second victories. They toss up more bull than three-pointers. And they wind up with more flak than rebounds. No superstar, no coach, no referee is safe from being victimized by these audacious jokesters. For "The Most Madcap Pranksters," The Basketball Hall of SHAME inducts the following:

LARRY BIRD

Forward ○ Boston Celtics ○ 1979–present

Larry Bird has a knack for keeping his team competitive on the court and loose in the locker room. That's because the Celtics' top scorer is also the club's top prankster.

"Larry is dead serious on the court, but behind the scenes, he's known as the guy who keeps things loose with his locker room pranks," said Boston sportswriter Mike Fine.

No one knows that better than former Celtics coach K. C. Jones. He was the target of a Bird practical joke during halftime in a critical late-season game in 1984.

With only a few minutes left to get his new strategy across to the team, Jones scribbled a new play on the blackboard and hurriedly pointed out first-half mistakes. He really wanted this victory and could feel the tension building in the locker room. After the coach made what he felt was a very important point, he noticed the players were acting strangely.

"It seemed to me the guys were all having mouth and face trouble," Jones recalled. "Their hands were rubbing their lips, chins, and cheeks. I later realized they were doing that to suppress their laughter. Anyway, I started to walk to the other side of the blackboard when I

had this terrible feeling that I couldn't move. I jolted to a stop and nearly fell flat on my face.

"I looked down and discovered that my shoelaces had been tied together. And there was Larry Bird right at my feet, grinning at me. That was the end of my halftime talk."

In 1984, rookie Rick Carlisle fell victim to a Bird prank. Club-house man Walter "Randy" Randall suspected that some of the players were stealing supplies. So Bird arranged to get eight pairs of new socks and had them stuffed in Carlisle's gym bag without the rookie's knowledge. Then Bird told Randall that Carlisle was swiping team socks. Moments later, as the unsuspecting rookie headed for the door, Randall stopped him, grabbed his bag, opened it, and found the socks. "Randy raised the roof," recalled Bird. "He went to tell the coach that Rick was a thief and naturally we're all laughing like crazy."

Dozing teammates are among Bird's favorite targets during flights. "One thing Larry loves to do is catch guys sleeping with their heads back on the seat," said Mike Fine. "Larry's known for sneaking up and poking wads of wet tissues up their noses."

Bird has left his mark in countless ways in the locker room. Teammates return from the showers to find their street clothes tied in knots, mashed sandwiches in their shoes, and orange peels and apple cores in their pockets. They don't even have to guess who did it. They know it's the work of Larry Bird, all-star prankster.

SCOTT HASTINGS

**Forward ○ New York Knicks–Atlanta Hawks–Miami Heat–Detroit Pistons
1982–present**

Throughout his NBA career, Scott Hastings has treated everyone the same. He's just as likely to pull a prank on an opposing player or official as he is on a teammate.

As a Detroit Piston, Hastings showed how sneaky—and brave—he was when he targeted huge Atlanta Hawks center Moses Malone in 1989 for a dirty trick.

When Malone arrived at The Palace, the Pistons' home arena, he realized he had left his sneakers back in his hotel room. So Malone collared a Detroit ball boy, tipped him $10, and sent the lad off to retrieve the shoes.

But Hastings had overheard Malone's instructions. The jokester intercepted the errand boy and paid him $20 to take his time. Meanwhile, Malone had to borrow a pair of high-tops from a teammate. Trainer Joe O'Toole chopped the shoes down into low-cuts for a better fit and colored in a Nike logo to meet the stipulations of Malone's contract with the shoe company.

Malone warmed up wearing the make-dos, expecting the ball boy to show up any minute with Moses' favorite game shoes. But the tip-off came and went. No shoes. Malone limped around in the shoddy shoes for most of the first quarter before the tardy ball boy finally reappeared with the right sneaks.

When asked by The Basketball Hall of SHAME to comment on the prank, Hastings said, "That's a true story, but I'm going to plead the Fifth Amendment on that one. If you've ever stood up close to Moses Malone, you'll know why I deny it. I might run into him again. Besides, I'm too cheap for a $20 practical joke. My pranks are more in the $1.98 and under range."

In fact, one of Hastings' favorite tricks is worth only a few cents.

"I like to 'penny' people in their hotel rooms," said Hastings. "I wait until some teammate has bolted his door and gone to bed. Then I sneak down the corridor to his room, push the door in as far as I can from the outside, and slide two or three pennies in between the wood and the door frame. That jams the bolt. It's almost impossible for the person inside to unbolt the door.

"When I was with Atlanta, I pennied [center] Tree Rollins in his room all the time. He'd have to call maintenance in the morning to get him out. It got so Tree would start leaving wake-up calls for 4 AM just to be sure he could get out of his room in time to catch the team bus."

But Rollins got his revenge. He pennied Hastings in the jokester's own room and then shot bottle rockets at him from under the door.

Hastings has never been afraid to stick it—literally—to the refs. When he joined the Pistons, he noticed that the players pass by the officials' dressing room going to and from the locker room. Suddenly, from the far reaches of his warped mind, Hastings conjured up a prank that he's pulled time and again.

Just before halftime, while sitting on the bench, he goes to work on a huge wad of bubble gum. "I mean, it's a big-time wad," said Hastings. "Then on the way to our locker room, I'll stick it under the door handle when we pass the officials' room. The first ref who gets there grabs the doorknob and you can hear the howls all the way to the end of the corridor."

Hastings' favorite targets are TV announcers. "I have this weird thing about play-by-play announcers," he said. "I can't bear to see them standing out there before the games looking so pretty and confident."

He loved to get Miami broadcaster Sam Smith and his sidekick, Eric Reid, when they were doing their live stand-up shots out on the court. While they were seen on TV from the shoulders up, Hastings often crawled over on his hands and knees, rolled their pants up to their knees, pulled their socks down, and sprayed an icy-feeling pain killer on their bare legs. Since they were on live, they had to keep smiling and pretend nothing was happening.

One time a scissors-wielding Hastings approached Smith, who was doing a live stand-up, and snipped off the announcer's tie just below camera level—and then returned before the live broadcast ended and cut off a second section.

"The first game of the year after I went to Detroit, I felt I just had to do something to make my mark," said Hastings. "So I crawled out and rolled [broadcaster] George Blaha's pants up. He was on live when I did it and he grumbled over the air, 'I hope Hastings is as good a player as he is a practical joker.' "

As the newest member of the Pistons in 1989, Hastings temporarily toned down the practical jokes around his teammates—at least until he checked out the Bad Boys' reputation for mayhem.

"Actually, I found the Pistons to be a fairly serious bunch of elderly gentlemen," said Hastings. "Since they were all hitting the geriatric level, I laid off some of the more action-oriented pranks like smoke bombs in their hotel rooms.

"But when everybody was accusing [center] Bill Laimbeer of being the dirtiest player in the league, I had a bunch of T-shirts made up saying 'Have you hugged Bill Laimbeer today?'

"I gave one to Bill, and he was very touched. First he hugged me. Then he stomped me."

KAREEM ABDUL-JABBAR

Center ○ Los Angeles Lakers ○ 1975–89

Kareem Abdul-Jabbar spent 20 years in the NBA picking off rebounds and picking up baskets. Then he started picking pockets as a prank—and drove teammate Byron Scott batty in the process.

Kareem was the first to admit that he made a better dunkster than dipster. But Kareem—known among his fellow players for his sly and low-key sense of humor—learned to pick pockets as a way of keeping his long fingers nimble and his Laker teammates entertained.

As the main target for his pocket-picking practice, Kareem zeroed in on Lakers guard Byron Scott, a prankster in good standing himself.

"Byron is the team's resident comedian," the superstar center recalled in his autobiography, *Kareem*. "For a while, I was practicing how to pick pockets with him as my victim. We would go on road trips and I would steal his pocket square or new hat. Or I would hide his dress shoes or try to take his jewelry—though I would warn anyone not to go for Byron's jewelry. You might lose a finger, or worse."

While all the Lakers learned to be on the lookout for Kareem's sticky-fingered pranks, it was Scott who constantly had to be on the alert and who knew just where to look whenever his hat, shoes, watch, or wallet was missing.

"Kareem always used to see what he could get away with," said Scott. "He'd pick my pockets, my bags, whatever else I had on the plane or the bus. He'd steal my hat, my gloves, the whole bit. We'd get to the hotel, or wherever we were headed, and when I went to get my stuff it would be gone. He even used to steal my shoes."

Once in Portland, recalled Scott, his regular shoes disappeared just as the team was leaving for dinner in the middle of a rainstorm. Scott had to dig his playing shoes out of his gym bag and wear them.

"It was either that or go barefooted," Scott said. "I was wearing a nice shirt, slacks, and a coat, so I looked pretty strange wearing playing shoes.

Andrew D. Bernstein/NBA Photos

"Kareem got so he could take the hankie right out of the breast pocket of my coat—while I was wearing it. Sometimes, to let me know he'd tricked me, Kareem would put it in his own breast pocket and wear it around for a couple of days. I'd see it and say, 'Hey, that looks just like mine. Hey! It *is* mine!' There were a few times when Kareem even managed to steal my hat and walk around wearing it. When I'd miss it, the first place I'd go was to Kareem.

"And he was always swiping my wallet. Never when I was asleep, though. Kareem always got me when I was wide awake.

"Kareem got so good at picking my pockets, he could have made a career out of it. But a 7-foot, 2-inch guy sneaking up on somebody would have been kind of noticeable."

A CROCK FULL OF (BOSTON) BEANS

Boston Celtics forward Kevin McHale pulled a fast one on his former college roommate, Chris Engler, who was playing against him for the first time in 1984 as a member of the New Jersey Nets.

Toward the end of the game, a Boston blowout, McHale whispered to Engler that he would let him move in close for an easy jumper. So Engler dribbled toward the basket and took the shot—and was shocked to have it slapped off his forehead by McHale.

"I thought you were going to give me the shot," a smarting Engler said to the Celtic.

Laughed McHale, "I lied."

DARRYL DAWKINS

Center ○ New Jersey Nets ○ 1983–84

Darryl Dawkins played his best when on the road. Not basketball but pranks.

The fun-loving Chocolate Thunder was an all-star jokester on team flights, especially during the 1983–84 season with the New Jersey Nets.

Heaven help those players foolish enough to snooze on the plane. Dawkins loved nothing better than to put shaving cream on the heads of slumbering teammates. Other times he tied their shoelaces together or cut their shirt buttons off while they dozed.

Dawkins' most memorable airborne prank happened 35,000 feet over the Midwest. His victim: 6-foot, 8-inch, 220-pound all-star forward Buck Williams.

Darryl had envied Williams' ability to nod off easily in unlikely places. When the team was on the road and a good night's sleep was hard to come by, Buck liked to catch quick catnaps wherever he could—on crowded buses to and from the airports, in noisy locker rooms, and, most of all, in cramped airline seats during flights. After much observation, Dawkins noticed that Williams often slept with his mouth wide open.

One night, on a cross-country flight, Darryl walked down the aisle and spotted Buck sawing logs with his head tilted back on the seat and his mouth wide open as usual.

"I could see clear down to his tonsils," recalled Dawkins.

With that cavern yawning before him, the prankster was struck by a sudden inspiration. Just how big, he wondered, was Buck Williams' mouth? "There's no better way to find out than by filling it up," thought Darryl.

Transformed into the mad scientist, Dawkins went in search of the items necessary for his experiment—all in the interest of medical science, of course.

First, he pulled out a huge cigar and eased it into Williams' open mouth. The subject hardly stirred in his sleep and the stogie barely filled the open space.

Andrew D. Bernstein/NBA Photos

As a crowd of interested Nets quietly gathered in the aisle to observe the experiment firsthand, a flight attendant who was recruited to help handed Darryl a big bunch of fresh grapes. Dawkins picked the fattest, juiciest grapes off the stem and packed them into Buck's mouth one at a time. Williams never twitched.

"I had to hand it to Buck," recalled Darryl. "He was one of the most cooperative victims I ever had the pleasure to work on."

Eventually, Williams' big mouth reached its limit. He stirred and began spitting out grapes. With the subject of the experiment now wide awake—and knowing how grumpy Buck could be when his sleep was disturbed—Dawkins and his chortling audience quickly scattered to their seats.

"None of us wanted to stick around to hear what Buck had to say about the grapes," recalled Darryl.

Unfortunately, the results of the test were lost. Dawkins failed to keep track of the exact number of grapes required to fill Buck Williams' mouth. Witnesses estimated between six and eight grapes. The only way to know for sure was to repeat the experiment . . . but no one was willing to test big Buck's patience again.

CLYDE LOVELLETTE

Center ○ St. Louis Hawks ○ Nov. 6, 1958

Big Clyde Lovellette pulled on his cowboy boots, slapped on his ten-gallon hat, strapped on his matched pair of six-shooters, and went gunning for referee Jim Duffy.

He shot him, too—sort of.

Lovellette and the St. Louis Hawks were on a western road trip during the 1958 exhibition season when he ran afoul of the veteran official during a game in Albuquerque, New Mexico.

"The officiating crew traveled with us on those exhibition trips," recalled Lovellette, "so we got to know each other pretty well and usually had a good time together off the court.

"But this one night, Duffy started calling fouls on me that I didn't think I deserved and he really got under my skin." Lovellette protested loudly and Duffy warned the Hawks' center to quiet down or he'd get a technical.

"I kept it up and, sure enough, Duffy hit me with a technical foul," Lovellette continued. "That really upset me, because this was just an exhibition game and nobody called technicals during exhibition season in those days."

Minutes later Duffy whistled another foul against Lovellette, which launched the big man into another tirade.

"If I have to call another technical on you, I'll throw you out of the game!" warned Duffy.

"I yelled back, 'If you throw me out of the game, I'll get you good,'" Lovellette recalled. "I didn't mean it and he knew it. We were always kidding like that. Nobody took it seriously."

But then a few minutes later Duffy called another foul on the Hawk's center, who then exploded in fury. Lovellette jumped all over him and the two waged a heated argument in the middle of the court. Duffy finally lost his notoriously short patience. "I've got no choice now," he shouted in Lovellette's face. "You're out of the game!"

Lovellette was stunned. "You can't do that, Duffy," he protested. "It's only an exhibition game and these people came to see me play."

But the banishment stuck and as Lovellette stalked off the floor, he pointed to the referee and yelled, "Duffy, I'll get you tonight."

At the time, westerns were the rage on television and their popularity had inspired a fast-draw craze. Lovellette and his roommate, Hub Reed, were caught up in the fad. They carried real six-guns with them on road trips and often practiced their fast-draw techniques before going to bed.

"That night after Duffy kicked me out of the game, Hub and I couldn't sleep," recalled Lovellette. "It was about 3 AM and we were still up practicing our fast draws.

"I said, 'Let's go get Duffy.' Hub tried to talk me out of it. He said it would just cause trouble, but I wouldn't listen. I was still smarting over being kicked out of the game, and I had this idea about getting even with Duffy."

Lovellette loaded his six-guns with blanks, grabbed his cowboy hat, and, with a fretting Hub Reed in his wake, stalked out into the dead-quiet night.

The team's motel was built in a horseshoe shape. Duffy was staying in a room across the wide-open courtyard from Lovellette's and Reed's room. As they stomped to Duffy's room, the two Hawks looked like old-time western villains heading for a showdown—except for one thing. They were still in their underwear.

A bright light over each door cast a spotlight glow over a portion of the courtyard. Lovellette took up a position in that light and told Reed to pound on Duffy's door.

"I almost had to drag Hub over there while I took up my quick-draw stance out in the courtyard," said Lovellette. "After Hub knocked a couple of times, we could hear Duffy in there grumbling and cussing about some fool waking him up in the middle of the night. He came to the door, threw it open really hard, and yelled, 'What the hell's going on here?'"

Reed leaped to one side and the only thing Duffy could see was a 6-foot, 9-inch, 240-pound giant, armed to the teeth, and silhouetted in the bright light.

Lovellette bellowed at the top of his voice, "You son of a bitch! I warned you that if you threw me out of the game I'd get you!"

Lovellette then whipped out his best fast draw—both six shooters at once—and blazed away with half a dozen shots in rapid fire. Duffy was so shocked by the startling sight and the ear-splitting roar of the six-guns that he fell back into the room and tumbled over the bed.

Reed was jumping up and down and screaming, "Damn, Clyde! You done killed him!"

"We ran into the room and flopped belly down across the bed," recalled Lovellette. "Duffy had his head stuck under the nightstand and was shaking like a leaf.

"When we saw he was OK, I grabbed Hub and pulled him out of the room. By now every light in the motel was on and people were running outside to see what all the gunfire was about. There were Hub and I running across the courtyard to get back to our own room. There wasn't any place to hide out there and we sure weren't going back in Duffy's room.

"So all those people were treated to the sight of two half-naked guys wearing six-guns, cowboy boots, and big ten-gallon hats, running through the night. I've never been more embarrassed in my life."

The next morning Duffy was out for revenge. He gleefully leaked word to the newspapers that some seminude giant closely resembling the St. Louis center had been spotted running through the motel parking lot in the wee hours of the morning carrying smoking six-guns.

The wire services pounced on the story and thereafter, whenever the Hawks arrived in a new city, Lovellette was besieged by the local press corps and questioned about the tawdry tale.

"I couldn't get away from that story all season," complained Lovellette. "Duffy loved seeing me squirm trying to explain why I was running around in the middle of the night wearing nothing but shorts and six-guns. I never lived it down.

"You know," he said with a laugh, "there were times when I wished I'd been packing real bullets."

BRAIN SPRAINS

Coaches and players have their head in the game every second of every period. They instantly size up the situation and know exactly what to do. Baloney! These guys daydream and get befuddled like the rest of us working stiffs. The only difference is that their office is the basketball court, and when they suffer a mental lapse, it usually spells disaster. For "The Most Mind-Boggling Mental Miscues," The Basketball Hall of SHAME inducts the following:

JAMES WORTHY
Forward ○ Los Angeles Lakers ○ May 31, 1984

ISIAH THOMAS
Guard ○ Detroit Pistons ○ May 26, 1987

The two costliest passes ever thrown in postseason play were made by all-stars who for one brief moment suffered a brain sprain that turned victory into crushing defeat.

Seconds away from knocking out the Boston Celtics in the Boston Garden in playoff games, superstars James Worthy of the Los Angeles Lakers and Isiah Thomas of the Detroit Pistons pulled a matched pair of snooze plays. At crucial turning points in both games, lackadaisical lobs by Worthy and Thomas landed right in the hands of Celtic defenders who turned the terrible tosses into game-saving baskets.

In the second game of the 1984 NBA Finals, the Lakers looked like winners. They held a 113–111 lead over the Celtics with 18 seconds left and had the ball in their possession. All they had to do was merely run out the clock to take a 2–0 advantage back to Los Angeles for game three.

Magic Johnson inbounded the ball to Worthy, who had three

options—pass back to Magic, dribble, or just stand there and wait to get fouled. But Worthy had other ideas.

He tossed a soft floater all the way across the court in the general direction of teammate Byron Scott. Boston's Gerald Henderson watched in amazement as the ball floated right to him. Henderson picked it off and took it to the hoop to tie the game with 13 seconds left. The stunned Lakers failed to get another shot off and the game went to overtime. Boston won in the extra period 124–121 to even the series at one game apiece.

"I won't be able to sleep tonight," moaned Worthy. "My vision wasn't in order. I just didn't see Henderson. The game should have been ours. This is very, very frustrating."

Meanwhile, the celebrating Henderson could hardly believe his good fortune. "Worthy threw the ball high," gloated Henderson. "He really hung it out there for me."

Said Laker Jamaal Wilkes as he trudged dejectedly out of the Boston Garden, "It probably will come back to haunt us." It did. Given an extra life thanks to Worthy's pass, the Celtics eventually captured the NBA championship four games to three.

History—and the luck of the Celtics—repeated itself during the 1987 Eastern Conference finals. This time it was Thomas' turn in the spotlight of shame when he snoozed with the Pistons just seconds away from winning.

The semifinal series was even at two games each. The Pistons were nursing a 107–106 lead with only five seconds remaining. If the score held up, the Pistons would take a three-games-to-two advantage back to the Silverdome, where they had pounded the Celtics to a pulp in two previous playoff games.

In the waning moments of the game, Larry Bird had just tried a shot for Boston, but it was blocked and bounced out of bounds off another Celtic. Downcourt, Pistons Dennis Rodman and Rick Mahorn were jumping up and down in celebration of impending victory.

Meanwhile, Thomas rushed to inbound the ball. He didn't see Detroit coach Chuck Daley frantically signaling from the other end of the court for a time-out. That would have given the Pistons the ball at halfcourt and time to set up a play to run out the clock.

Instead, Thomas lofted a lazy pass to Bill Laimbeer in the back court. But Bird, who was expecting to foul Laimbeer to give the Celtics one more chance at a three-point play, leaped in front of the Pistons' center and snatched the ball away.

Bird then flipped the ball to an alert Dennis Johnson, who was streaking for the basket. Johnson laid it in and the Celtics pulled off another miracle finish with a 108–107 victory.

A stunned Isiah Thomas collapsed at courtside in disbelief. Later, Thomas admitted he had dozed off at the worst possible time. "I just didn't see him coming," Thomas said of Bird's easy steal. "I was just trying to get the ball in quick so they'd have to foul us."

For Bird, it was like taking candy from a baby. "I don't know what Isiah was thinking about. He just kind of lobbed the ball up there for Laimbeer and I took it."

The Celtics also took the conference series, four games to three, and won the right to meet the Los Angeles Lakers in the NBA Finals, which L.A. won.

A few months later, Isiah said, "It's a pass I never want to forget, simply because if you don't learn from your mistakes, if you don't take the bad with the good, then you're not a man."

NOT MAKING THE GRADE

Kentucky coach Eddie Sutton had more than one reason to be upset following the Wildcats' 1988 loss to Auburn.

He wanted to find out exactly where his players' heads were, so he gave them a pop quiz. The results indicated he had a few airheads on the team.

Fewer than half the players could name the player who made the winning basket for Auburn (John Caylor), the final score (53–52), or Kentucky's next three opponents.

KORY HALLAS

Guard ○ Eastern Michigan Hurons ○ March 11, 1989

As the final seconds ticked away, Kory Hallas drove down the lane and scored an uncontested basket. He thrust his fist into the air in celebration of tying the score and forcing the game into overtime.

Then Hallas glanced at the scoreboard . . . and fell to his knees in shock. His team, the Eastern Michigan Hurons, had trailed the Ball State Cardinals by *three* points, not two as he had thought before making the buzzer-beater. The only significance his basket had was that Eastern Michigan lost by one point instead of three.

Unfortunately for Hallas and his team, the snooze play happened at the worst possible time. It eliminated the 16–13 Hurons from the Mid-American Conference tournament and sent Ball State (27–2) to the finals with a narrow 77–76 victory.

Hallas' brain sprain was even more embarrassing since the sharp-shooter usually was a deadeye on three-point shots. In fact, his three-point basket with 1:36 left in the game had shaved Ball State's lead to 74–73 and had moved Eastern Michigan into position to upset the favored Cardinals.

The Hurons trailed by a single point until four seconds remained when Ball State's Paris McCurdy sank a pair of free throws to give the Cardinals a 77–74 lead.

The only chance Eastern Michigan had was to attempt a three-point basket. A long, inbounds pass went to Hallas just across mid-court. He turned and dribbled for the basket with only one player, Billy Butts, guarding him. But Hallas didn't pull up at the three-point line as everyone in the arena expected. He drove for the layup—while the surprised Butts stood aside and watched him go.

"I was playing him for the three-point shot," recalled Butts. "When he crossed the line, I just let him go. I wasn't about to stop him if that's what he wanted to do."

After scoring what he thought was the tying basket, Hallas danced with joy while his teammates looked on in stunned disbelief. When Hallas saw the scoreboard and realized his gaffe, he crumbled to his knees and later had to be helped off the floor.

"I thought it was weird that they [the Cardinals] were celebrating and we weren't," recalled a mortified Hallas.

"I just forgot the score. I got the ball and there was an opening so I took it to the hole. I looked up at the scoreboard expecting to see the score tied. Instead we were down by one and the game was over."

Eastern Michigan coach Ben Braun called the blunder "a human mistake." Added the coach, "Hallas was obviously upset. It would have been a tough shot but he could have taken it. He had made three-pointers before in the game. And this one time we really needed it."

After the game, Hallas told reporters, "I hate to see the season end that way. It's going to take me a long time to forget this one."

WEST VIRGINIA MOUNTAINEERS

Jan. 11, 1990

During a time-out late in a crucial game, the West Virginia Mountaineers became so engrossed in talking basketball that they momentarily forgot about playing basketball.

And while the Mountaineers were still huddled in their courtside confab, the Temple Owls casually inbounded the ball and canned a freebie lay-up on a bizarre 5-on-0 break.

The basket broke a tie and, as a result, the team that was so lost in thought lost the game.

When the Owls arrived in Morgantown to meet the Mountaineers, the two teams were locked in a tie for first place in the Atlantic 10 Conference. As expected, the game in noisy old McGonigle Hall, West Virginia's 4,100-seat gym, went down to the wire.

With 3:10 left to play and the score knotted at 66–66, Temple called time-out. Both teams gathered around their coaches to plot strategy. At the end of the time-out period, a warning horn sounded. According to the rules, the teams have 15 seconds to return to the court before a second horn sounds and play resumes.

But the Mountaineers remained bunched around Coach Gale Catlett through the first warning horn as well as the 15-second grace period. They still hadn't budged when the final warning sounded.

Meanwhile, the Owls were on the floor ready and waiting to play. So referee John Clougherty signaled the timekeeper to start the clock. Temple's Mark Macon took the inbound pass, went downcourt uncontested, and slammed home the go-ahead dunk.

The howls of protest from the hometown crowd snapped the Mountaineers out of their slumber. West Virginia raced back on the court, but too late to stop the easy bucket—or save the game. They never recovered from Temple's critical basket and lost 73–69.

Catlett argued that he couldn't hear the warning horn over the crowd noise. But the officials pointed out that Temple had no trouble hearing the horn. Besides, added the refs, McGonigle was the Mountaineers' home court. They should have been used to the noise.

Later, Catlett filed a protest over the controversial call, but his plea was rejected and the game went into the record books as a defeat for the Mountaineers.

West Virginia's director of sports information, Shelly Poe, complained that the referees hadn't taken the time to alert the preoccupied Mountaineers.

"The coach was flabbergasted," said Poe. "We weren't even out of the huddle yet. All of a sudden, Temple was going in for a lay-up and our guys had to race down to the other end to get the ball back in play before we were called for delay of game.

"The game was tied at that point and we were playing for first place in the conference. In a game that important, it didn't seem fair that they'd start playing without us."

Temple coach John Chaney showed some sympathy for West Virginia's beef. "It's like your car got a ticket for being parked in front of the hospital while you were in the emergency room," said Chaney.

SAY WHAT?

• Longtime Los Angeles announcer Chick Hearn said one of his most mortifying moments on the air came while calling a college basketball game in Arizona. "I intended to say, 'He hit the shot,' but it came out, 'He shit the hot.' Another time, while I was doing a TV game with the Lakers, a guy forgot to turn down the mike during a commercial. A player had just made six bad plays in a row. I said something like, 'Why don't they get that dumb son of a bitch out of there?'" His remark was broadcast for all to hear.

• In a 1972 game, the lowly Cleveland Cavaliers had the ball and trailed the Baltimore Bullets 110–108 when Cleveland's Dave Sorenson nailed a tying buzzer-beater. Cavs play-by-play man Joe Tait was so excited he shouted, "Cavs win, 110–110!"

• In a 1983 game, the Denver Nuggets were getting beat by 25 points when Mike Evans hit a three-pointer at the end of the third quarter. "It was a good shot but there was no value to it," recalled Nuggets play-by-play man Jeff Kingery. "I wanted to say something like, 'That's about as good as throwing a stone in the ocean.' But what I said was, 'That's about as good as taking a piss in the ocean.'"

• Brent Musburger was working a Chicago Bulls game in 1976 when he mistakenly said Bulls forward Bob Love was the brother of the Beach Boys' Mike Love. The two Loves are not related. Besides, Bob is black, Mike is white.

"Oscar Robertson was my analyst," Musburger recalled. "He gave me a weird, weird look but didn't say anything. I knew something was wrong, but I didn't know what. Then at halftime, someone said to me, 'You must know something about the Beach Boys no one else does.' That's when it hit me. It was another player, Stan Love, who was Mike's brother.

"I was really embarrassed and I told Oscar, 'This is one I'm not going to correct on the air because I can only make it worse. But I'll answer all letters and calls.' Do you know that I didn't get one letter or call. I began wondering, 'Wasn't anyone watching?' "

CHICAGO BULLS

April 15, 1973

The Chicago Bulls' 1973 title hopes passed away in more ways than one.

The Bulls had a golden opportunity to dethrone the defending champion Los Angeles Lakers in the Western Conference semifinals. But Chicago let the chance pass by.

Incredibly, in their final possession of the game, the Bulls, who were trailing by just one point, kept passing the ball back and forth to each other and ran out the 24-second clock without taking a shot!

"It was absolutely unbelievable," recalled Chicago coach Dick Motta. "It would have been a bitter loss to have missed the shot. But to not even have taken a shot . . ."

The Bulls were leading throughout the seventh and deciding game, which was played at the Forum in Los Angeles, but the Lakers rallied in the final minutes. With 26 seconds left, L.A. scored to grab a 93–92 lead.

Chicago moved the ball across the midcourt line and called time-out with 19 seconds to play and 17 seconds remaining on the shot clock. The Bulls then gathered around Motta to set up the final, game-winning play. The coach told them to work the ball into Chet Walker and leave enough time for a possible rebound.

When Chicago inbounded the ball, Motta watched in horror as the Bulls passed and passed—but forgot to shoot. The ball went to Walker, who passed off to Bob Weiss in the corner. He passed back out to Jerry Sloan. The seconds were ticking away. The players just stood around and passed.

With each "passing" second, the crowd screamed louder and the tension intensified. A desperate Motta leaped to his feet and shouted the time from the shot clock: "Five! . . . Four! . . . Three!"

Meanwhile, Assistant Coach Phil Johnson was yelling, "Shoot the ball! Shoot!"

Like the others, Sloan passed up the chance to take a shot and passed off to Bob Love in the key. The ball reached Love's hands just as the buzzer signaled that the 24-second clock had expired.

With two seconds remaining, Chicago's Norm Van Lier hit the Lakers' Jerry West with a flying tackle. West sank a pair of game-icing free throws and the Lakers won 95–92 to capture the seven-game semifinal series.

"We were stunned," recalled Motta. "There was nothing to say. We knew we had to chew this one before we could swallow it. We sat chewing and the taste was bad.

"I finally told them, 'It was a hell of a way to lose a season.' It was strange, but we had no goat. Either we were all to blame or no one was. In the play where we could have scored, everyone had handled the ball. We shared the humiliation."

"T"-TOTALERS

They rant and rave . . . hoot and holler . . . boil and burn. It's usually only a matter of time before hotheaded players or coaches say or do something so offensive that the ref signals his disapproval, technically speaking. Getting hit with a technical foul silences most temper tantrums . . . but not necessarily all the outrageous ones. For "The Most Audacious Technical Fouls," The Basketball Hall of SHAME inducts the following:

MITCH BUONAGURO

Coach ○ Fairfield University Stags ○ March 2, 1988

Mitch Buonaguro's ecstasy caused his team's agony.

The excitable coach of the Fairfield University Stags celebrated an apparent victory just one second too soon. As a result, he was given a technical for running onto the court before the game was over. The last-second technical foul shots turned the Stags' thrilling win into a shocking loss.

The underdog Stags made a surprisingly strong showing against the St. Peter's Peacocks in the opening round of the 1988 Metro Atlantic Athletic Conference tournament. As the final seconds ticked off the clock, Fairfield's Harold Brantley grabbed a 50-foot crosscourt pass and scored to give the Stags what appeared to be an amazing 60–59 triumph.

At least Coach Buonaguro believed his team had won. He joyously dashed to midcourt, leaped in the air, and did a victory dance with his players.

But St. Peter's coach Ted Fiore wasn't giving up without a fight. He did his own war dance around the referees. He reminded them that St. Peter's had called time with one second left. And he convinced them that Buonaguro had violated the rules because time hadn't expired when he ran out to embrace his players.

After a long debate, the officials decided in Fiore's favor. A technical was called against Buonaguro for leaving the coaching box and celebrating too early. The refs handed the ball to Willie Haynes, St. Peter's best free throw shooter. While the livid Buonaguro was being restrained by his two assistant coaches, Haynes made both technical foul shots (a "T" is a two-shot foul in the college game) to regain the lead for St. Peter's, 61–60.

The Peacocks then got possession following the free throws. When they inbounded, Troy Bradford was fouled with the clock still showing one second to go. Bradford made both of his free throws and St. Peter's miraculously escaped with a 63–60 win.

Buonaguro complained that Fiore also had left the coaching box to go jaw at the officials and should have been called for the same violation.

"We lost the game on a call that shouldn't have been made," stormed Buonaguro in the locker room. "My team won the game on a basket with one second left. I'm an emotional guy. I thought the game was over so I ran onto the court. Now I'm sick about it. I've probably never been this sick before."

But Fiore insisted he was just playing by the rules. "It was as much of a rules infraction as walking or charging," said Fiore. "Buonaguro was obviously out on center court and the game wasn't over. My gut feeling was that the officials weren't going to make the call, so I brought it to their attention.

"I'm not embarrassed about winning that way at all. But I guess if I was the other coach I would be sick."

And while the argument raged around him, a stunned Harold Brantley, who thought he'd won the game with his last-second heroics, sat on the bench holding his head.

"I feel like I'm in the Twilight Zone," said Brantley. "I'm waiting for someone to wake me up and tell me we won."

DICK MOTTA

Coach ○ Chicago Bulls ○ Feb. 21, 1971

JIM BARNETT

Guard ○ Golden State Warriors ○ Dec. 18, 1973

Dick Motta and Jim Barnett lofted the highest, most outrageous punts in NBA history.

Both boots ended in technicals. But, incredibly, Motta got away with his—because the refs punished the opposing coach instead!

The visiting Chicago Bulls were trailing the Detroit Pistons by two points in the closing minute of a 1971 game when Chicago's Jerry Sloan drove for the basket. His shot was batted away by Pistons center Otto Moore, who was called for a foul.

But Motta leaped off the bench, protesting that Moore had swatted the shot on its downward arc and should be called for goaltending. However, the refs ignored the enraged coach because they were trying to halt a shoving match between the two players under the basket.

AP/Wide World Photos

In the confusion, the ball was tossed aside and bounced straight to Motta, who was standing and shouting by the bench. The coach, incensed that the officials had missed the goaltending call, caught the ball and suddenly saw a golden opportunity to express his aggravation.

Motta then turned toward the stands at Cobo Hall, dropped the ball, and booted it as hard as he could. "The thrust of my beautiful punt lifted me right off the ground in a follow-through that would have thrilled [Chicago Bears coach] George Halas," Motta recalled. "The ball soared a good 30 yards into the second balcony. It dropped right into the hands of a fan who must have weighed 300 pounds.

"I knew before the ball got to him that I had made a terrible mistake. I backed up to the bench and sat on my hands, looking the other way."

Bulls reserve center Jim Fox gasped in disbelief at Motta, who was trying to act as if nothing had happened. "Coach, I didn't see you do that," said Fox. "Tell me I didn't see you do that."

By then, the officials had quelled the disturbance on the floor and went looking for the game ball. Players on the Detroit bench were on their feet pointing at Motta and then up into the balcony, where arena security officers were recovering the unexpected punt from the surprised fan.

Incredibly, neither official had seen Motta kick the ball. When it became obvious they weren't going to charge the Chicago coach with a technical for his flagrant behavior, Detroit coach Butch van Breda Kolff was outraged. He raced onto the floor to protest the oversight to referee Don Murphy.

"Did you see that?" shouted van Breda Kolff.

"No, Coach," replied the referee. "I definitely did not see him kick the ball into the stands."

"Well I'm not surprised, you blind bastard," retorted the fuming coach. "You haven't gotten anything else right out here tonight."

That earned van Breda Kolff a quick technical foul. While Cobo Hall erupted in boos, a chaste Motta sat on the bench, trying hard to suppress a grin.

"I was furious," recalled van Breda Kolff. "Mainly because I'd always wanted to punt a ball into the stands during a game, but Motta beat me to it."

Nearly three years later, Golden State Warriors guard Jim Barnett kicked an even longer punt during a game against the Buffalo Braves.

His boot landed in the third-tier seats of the Oakland Coliseum Arena.

It happened after referee Ed Batogowski had called Barnett for fouling the Braves' Randy Smith in the act of shooting. "I was stunned," recalled Barnett. "I was four feet away from Randy when I was called for the foul. I staggered around the court, shaking my head and pantomiming how the refs were picking on poor little me."

The second official, Mendy Rudolph, didn't care for Barnett's act and flashed the "T" sign at him. Barnett decided to retaliate.

"As Batogowski was handing the ball to Randy to shoot the technical, I just plucked it right out of the ref's hands and, still in full stride, punted the ball as hard as I could. It flew way up into the cheap seats on the third level. I mean, I got my whole foot into it. Some kid caught the ball right by an exit and took off with it. They had to go find a new ball and that delayed the game for several minutes."

Meanwhile, the Mad Punter never lost a step. Knowing he would get a second technical, which meant automatic ejection, Barnett marched off the floor and straight to the locker room. "I never looked back after kicking the ball," recalled Barnett. "As I left the court, I got a standing ovation and went out waving and bowing to my adoring fans.

"But after the game, I started getting worried. I knew I'd get a big fine. So I went to the officials' room to talk to Mendy. The first thing he said was, 'Hey, hotshot, in all my years in the league, I've never seen one kicked further.'"

Like all players who were called for technicals, Barnett later received a notice from the refs specifying the nature of the "T" and the amount of the fine. "I received two slips," he recalled. "One showed a technical for mocking the refs. The second notice was for kicking the ball into the seats. Mendy had put down a $500 fine. But then he crossed it out and penciled in 'free kick.'"

"T" AND SYMPATHY

When Indiana coach Bobby Knight launched into a tirade against the refs during a 1972 game against the University of Texas–El Paso, he drew three technicals in almost as many seconds and automatically was ejected.

On his way out of the arena under escort of a Pinkerton guard,

Mike Fender/*The Indianapolis News*

Knight asked his assistant, Dave Bliss, "What are you going to do now?"

"I don't know," Bliss replied. "But they are going to shoot about 100 technical foul shots and that will give me 20 minutes to think of something."

WARD "PIGGY" LAMBERT

Coach ○ Purdue Boilermakers ○ Feb. 18, 1933

Purdue coach Piggy Lambert stole a victory from his own team by getting a technical for literally mugging an opposing player in the final minute of a nip-and-tuck game.

Piggy was an excitable man who never backed down from anything or anyone. His pugnacity, coupled with his nervous habit of failing to sit still on the bench, often got him into trouble with the referees.

But Piggy never cost his team a victory until the day the Boilermakers battled the Ohio State Buckeyes in 1933 before a packed house in Columbus. It was one of the most bitterly fought games of the year, which pushed the high-strung coach to the brink of losing control.

With about 30 seconds left to play, the Boilermakers trailed the Buckeyes 27–25 when Norm Cottom, Purdue's All-America forward, stole the ball and raced downcourt. It looked for sure as though he would make a game-tying lay-up.

But Buckeyes guard Bill Beitner sprinted in hot pursuit, caught the Boilermaker just as he was about to score, and knocked Cottom into the next county.

Ohio State's Bobby Colburn, who was trailing the play, recalled, "It was a class A foul. Cottom sailed clear up into the stands. The next thing I knew, the Purdue coach was out on the floor, yelling and waving his arms."

When Cottom flew off the court, Piggy Lambert flew off the handle. In a fit of rage, the wild-eyed coach raced after Beitner, leaped on the startled player, and wanted to choke him. Referee Dave Reese and most of Beitner's teammates had to pry Lambert off the Buckeye's back and shove him to his own bench.

Just a split second before Piggy went to pieces, Reese had called Beitner for the obviously deliberate foul on Cottom. But the ref couldn't ignore Lambert's attempted assault and battery, so he hit the coach with a technical for charging onto the floor.

Cottom sank both his free throws to tie the game at 27–27. But then Bobby Colburn went to the line and made the technical foul for Ohio State that put the Buckeyes back on top by one point. Ohio State gained possession of the ball and ran out the clock, squeaking by with a 28–27 victory.

Said the *Columbus Journal Dispatch,* "Had Lambert kept quiet or had some cooler-headed Purdue partisan succeeded in handcuffing him to the bench, the score would have been tied." And the Boiler-makers might not have lost the game.

HIGH POINT COLLEGE PANTHERS
Feb. 10, 1988

It didn't seem possible, but the High Point College Panthers made a last-second, tie-breaking basket—and *lost*.

Incredibly, what should have been a dramatic high point turned into a heartbreaking low point for the team. All because of a rare game-ending technical foul.

The Panthers (15–4) were battling Carolinas Conference rival the Elon College Fighting Christians (16–6). The score was tied 59–59 as Elon played for the last shot. But with six seconds left in the game, High Point guard George Byers made a sensational steal of a sloppy Elon bounce pass and raced down the court.

Byers leaped high in the air and slammed the ball home for the go-ahead basket. The referee immediately blew his whistle, stopping the clock with just one second to play. The Panthers thought they had won 61–59. But the official had some good news and some bad news for them.

First came the good news: the basket counted. Then came the bad news: the ref had whistled Byers for charging into Elon guard Tony Chavis on the lay-up. Next came the really bad news: High Point forward Hugh Gelston, skying for a possible rebound, had acciden-tally grabbed the basket on the way down and was given a technical foul for hanging onto the rim.

That meant the Panthers' apparent game-winning shot actually had given the Fighting Christians a chance to win the game!

Chavis went to the charity stripe for a one-and-one. He made the first free throw, but missed the second. Then Elon's Brian Branson stepped to the line and canned the one-shot technical to tie the score at 61–61.

The game went into overtime . . . and the High Point players went into shock. Given new life, the Fighting Christians skinned the Pan-thers 77–71.

"We were less than a heartbeat away from beating them," sighed High Point coach Jerry Steele. "But we blew it. I couldn't believe so much could happen and the whole game could go down the tubes in just one measly second."

Amazingly, Elon found out for itself when the two teams met a month later and battled to a tie in regulation play. Then with just two seconds left in overtime, and High Point trailing 91–88, Elon's Brian Branson was fouled and went to the line.

The crowd was already singing "Goodbye, High Point," with good reason. Branson had hit 34 straight free throws. But his shot bounced off the rim and into the hands of High Point guard Chris Windlan. He took three dribbles and hurled the ball 67 feet. The buzzer sounded just as the ball swished through the net. The desperation three-point shot tied the game and sent it into double overtime.

The stunned Fighting Christians, already savoring a win, couldn't muster a comeback in the second extra period, and the Panthers had their revenge: 99–95.

BOB KAUFFMAN

Guard ○ Buffalo Braves ○ March 9, 1974

Bob Kauffman discovered that imitating referees draws laughs from fans—but technicals from officials.

His buffoonery didn't seem all that funny when it ended up costing his team a victory.

The Buffalo Braves (forerunners of the Los Angeles Clippers) were playing at home against the Seattle SuperSonics in front of a large, pumped-up crowd when Braves guard Ernie DiGregorio was called for dribbling out of bounds.

Buffalo immediately called time-out and Kauffman, the Braves' captain who had yet to enter the game, ran onto the court to beef at referee Lee Jones, who had made the call. The floor debate raged on until the second official, Richie Powers, moved in and ordered Kauffman back to the bench.

Powers turned away, but suddenly the 16,218 Buffalo fans started hooting. When he looked back, Powers saw Kauffman prancing around behind Jones, mocking the referee's peculiar stiff-legged gait.

Powers rushed back to defend his partner's honor and barked at Kauffman, "You're going way beyond the acceptable behavior. Mimicking a referee is not one of your jobs as captain of the team. Now knock it off and get back to your bench."

But as Powers walked away the second time, Kauffman resumed his burlesque act—only this time the target of his mocking impersonation was Richie Powers. Kauffman circled the referee, copying Powers' strut, to the great delight of the crowd.

Powers was fuming. He blew his whistle and signaled a technical against Kauffman. "That's one!" shouted the miffed ref. "The second one is coming if you don't shut up and sit down now!"

But Kauffman kept berating the officials and an instant later Powers kept his promise. The second "T" brought an automatic ejection and a quick, inglorious end to Kauffman's impersonations. As the steaming Kauffman stomped off the court to the cheers of a now raucous crowd, the SuperSonics sank both technical foul shots— points that would prove to be crucial later on.

For Powers, it was the first and only time in his long career that he had ever ejected a team captain who had not yet been in the game.

Both referees knew they would have to put up with Kauffman-inspired boos, jeers, and hoots from the frenzied fans. As luck would have it, moments after sending Kauffman to the showers, Powers called a foul against Buffalo. Then he spotted Braves publicist Rudy Martzke at courtside, screaming invectives over the ref's call, which only incited the crowd even more. Powers stopped the game, went to the sideline, and gave Martzke the heave-ho.

A smattering of fans began to chant, "Powers is a bum! Powers is a bum!" Then, like a tidal wave gaining speed and power, thousands upon thousands of incensed Braves boosters picked up the chant and roared, "Powers is a bum!" in ear-ringing unison that rocked Memorial Auditorium.

And it had all been instigated by Kauffman's theatrics, which seemed cute and funny in the first quarter. But they looked just the opposite by the end of the game. That's because the foul shots from Kauffman's two technicals helped Seattle tie the game at the end of regulation time. Buffalo then lost in overtime 123–117.

BILLY TUBBS

Coach ○ Oklahoma Sooners ○ Feb. 9, 1989

Billy Tubbs found out there are definite limits to freedom of speech. He was hit with a technical foul while making a public announcement.

The referees had asked the Oklahoma Sooners coach to get on the

PA and help quiet thousands of unruly Oklahoma fans angered over an official's call. So Tubbs grabbed the microphone and complied—but added his own editorial comment about the "terrible" officiating.

As Tubbs finished speaking, a red-faced ref was signaling the "T."

Tubbs' sly zebra-bashing performance was broadcast over national television and witnessed by the largest crowd in Oklahoma basketball history. They, along with 130 sportswriters, were on hand to watch the fifth-ranked Sooners (19–3) take on the third-ranked Missouri Tigers (20–3) with first place in the Big Eight Conference at stake.

The Tigers jumped out to a quick 18–5 lead, when Tubbs, well known for his sideline ref rantings, turned up the volume on his whine machine. The coach's gyrations in front of the bench only helped fire up an already inflamed crowd of 11,734 Sooner fans—5,000 of whom were armed with toy megaphones that had been handed out at the gate.

With 15:29 to go in the first half, Tubbs loudly protested an out-of-bounds call that went against Oklahoma. He then picked up his first technical for continuing the tirade through a television time-out.

When play resumed, the irate Sooner fans—incited by the coach's ravings—showed their disgust at the officiating by showering the court with the toy megaphones and other debris. Fearing a budding riot, referee Ed Hightower asked Tubbs to speak to the crowd and calm everyone down so the game could continue.

Tubbs grabbed the microphone and stepped out onto the court. An expectant hush fell over the throng.

"The referees," Tubbs announced, "have asked that, regardless of how terrible the officiating is, please don't throw things on the floor."

The words were barely out of his mouth before the bedlam

resumed, more frenzied than ever. With a smug look on his face, Tubbs handed the mike back to Hightower, who in return handed Tubbs his second technical within 40 seconds.

"I didn't think I'd get a technical for that," Tubbs said later. "I just did what the officials asked me to do." After further reflection, he added, "I guess if I had to do it all over again, I would've said some things differently."

But Tubbs had already made his point. Seven of the next eight personal fouls were called against the Tigers as the Sooners went on a 15–4 scoring spree that catapulted them to a 112–105 victory.

For his moment of microphone madness, Tubbs earned a special award. *Referee* magazine named him its "Bush League Coach of the Century."

DUNK YOU VERY MUCH

They fly through the air with the greatest of ease / And can bust a backboard whenever they please. / They love to toast their monster jams / With high fives and body slams. / But there are times when their slam dunks / Leave them in red-faced funks. / Whenever they soar but still muff it / Fans will be the first to shout, "Stuff it!"

For "The Most Inglorious Slams," The Basketball Hall of SHAME inducts the following:

NANCY REAGAN

First Lady ○ Feb. 4, 1988

It was the easiest dunk in the world. Even a baby could have made it. With Charles Barkley and Wayman Tisdale holding her up, Nancy Reagan attempted her first NBA dunk—and blew it!

The 5-foot, 1-inch First Lady suffered her moment of basketball shame during a trip to Indianapolis. She went there to show her support for the Clean Team, an antidrug program organized by the Indiana Pacers and Tisdale, their star forward.

To promote the event, the White House arranged for Mrs. Reagan to appear at halftime of the Pacers—Philadelphia 76ers game in Market Square Arena where, with a lift from Tisdale and the Sixers' Barkley, she would dunk the ball.

To make sure there weren't any unexpected glitches, White House aides and Secret Service agents insisted on carefully choreographing the stunt beforehand.

"I met Mrs. Reagan earlier in the day at a high school where we were both appearing," recalled Tisdale. "Barkley wasn't there but the Secret Service made me practice lifting her up by myself anyway.

"She kept calling me Wayne and saying things like, 'Now don't

Mike Fender/*The Indianapolis News*

drop me, Wayne.' So of course the first thing that happened was that I almost dropped her and there were these 50 Secret Service guys all around us ready to drop me if I did."

Tisdale said he made it through the rehearsal without dropping the First Lady but then had to face the ordeal of doing it for real in front of a packed arena that night.

"Since Barkley hadn't practiced with us, he was real nervous about what to do," recalled Tisdale. "I was nervous, she was nervous, and that made the Secret Service nervous—which made Barkley and me even more nervous."

In front of 14,054 fans, the two players lifted Mrs. Reagan up so she could just drop the ball through the hoop. But, obviously influenced by the flashy dunks she had seen in the first half, the First Lady got carried away. She tried a jam—and missed. The ball bounced off the rim as the crowd tittered and politely kept from bursting into laughter.

"Barkley and I looked at each other and kind of rolled our eyes like, 'Oh no! We're going to be here all night,'" recalled Tisdale. "We could hear people up in the stands start giggling and I was scared to death I'd start laughing too. I mean, how could she miss it when all she had to do was drop it in the basket?"

Mrs. Reagan insisted on one more try. Tisdale and Barkley picked her up a second time and held her high above the rim so she wouldn't blow the shot again. To the loud cheers of the crowd, the First Lady made it on her second attempt.

Recalled Tisdale, "She later told me, 'I would have made the first one except I was too nervous.' She was nervous? Man, she didn't know the half of it. All I could think of was, What's the Secret Service going to do if we drop her? Thank goodness, she was a little bitty thing. It would have been awful if she'd been a fat First Lady."

DARRYL DAWKINS

Center ○ Philadelphia 76ers ○ Nov. 13, 1979 and Dec. 5, 1979

Darryl Dawkins slammed his way into the NBA rule book.

The man they called the Master of Disaster, Chocolate Thunder, Sir Slam, Dr. Dunk, and Demon of Destiny destroyed two backboards with monster jams in the span of 22 days.

At the rate he was going, the slam man would have wiped out every backboard in the league before the end of the season had not the

AP/Wide World Photos

commissioner's office immediately instituted a new rule that all NBA backboards be equipped with collapsible rims.

When he became the first high school player to jump straight into the NBA in 1975, Dawkins announced with tongue in cheek that his greatest ambition was to bust backboards. But Double D shocked everybody, including himself, when he actually demolished his first one during a game against the Kings in Kansas City's Memorial Stadium on Nov. 13, 1979.

The 6-foot, 11-inch, 265-pound dunkateer brought the house down—or at least part of it—after making a routine power move to the hoop against Kings center Bill Robinzine 38 seconds into the second half. When The Dawk hit the two-handed jam, the board exploded like a bomb had gone off. Chunks of glass rained down on Dawkins and Robinzine, who both ducked for cover and then brushed shards of glass off their heads. "My first thought was that it was time to get out of Dodge," said Dawkins.

Players on both benches, who were safely out of range, watched in open-mouthed amazement. The 10,000 fans were so stunned they were silent at first. No one knew what to make of what they had just witnessed. When it sank in, players stood off to the side and shook with laughter.

It took over an hour for a maintenance crew to sweep up the glass and replace the board. When one worker gloated that he was going to sell the pieces as souvenirs, Dawkins started grabbing the bigger chunks for himself.

Kings general manager Joe Axelson was furious over the destructive dunk. "He was so upset," said Dawkins, "that he wanted me to pay for the broken glass, about $300."

Fortunately, no one was injured except for Robinzine, who suffered a slight cut on his hand. However, he did receive a massive wound to the ego when his name became part of the moniker for the infamous dunk. Dawkins called the spectacular smash his Chocolate Thunder Flyin', Robinzine Cryin', Teeth Shakin', Glass Breakin', Rump Roastin', Bun Toastin', Wham, Bam, I Am Jam!

Over the next few games, he wowed spectators with his powerful but nondestructive dunks and gave them colorful names such as the In Your Face Disgrace, Lefthanded Spine-Chiller Supreme, Sexophonic Turbo Delight, Cover Your Damn Head, Look Out Below, and the Greyhound Bus Dunk (in honor of the rare times Dawkins went coast to coast to score).

Fans everywhere wondered if the Incredible Dunk would ever wipe out another backboard again. They didn't have to wait long. Only 22 days after the immortal K.C. slam, Dawkins performed another rim-wrecking, board-busting jam when the Sixers played the visiting San Antonio Spurs in the Spectrum on December 5.

Dawkins was alone under the basket when he took a pass and slammed the ball with such force that he ripped the hoop right off the backboard. "I didn't mean to destroy it," said Dawkins. "It was the power, the Chocolate Thunder. I could feel it surging through my body, fighting to get out. I had no control."

He named the slam his No Playin', Get Out of the Wayin', Backboard Swayin', Game Delayin' Dunk.

Dawkins' jam topped his previous personal record for delaying the game. It took the Philadelphia crew one hour and 14 minutes to install a new board, or four minutes longer than the replacement time in Kansas City.

Dawkins' dunks were so awesome that reporters formed betting pools on the date of his next board buster. One official from another team even hinted that it would help attendance if the hometown fans knew that Dawkins would promise a shattering replay when he visited their arena.

But Commissioner Larry O'Brien quickly put a stop to any future hoop hoopla when he called Dawkins on the carpet. The commissioner warned Sir Slam to silence his Chocolate Thunder or else pay dearly in the pocketbook. O'Brien then ordered that all NBA backboards be equipped with collapsible rims. That way, nobody will ever smash a backboard again, he declared.

"I guess if I got any satisfaction from all this," said Dawkins, "it's knowing that I did more for job safety in the NBA than all of the Occupational Safety and Health Administration regulations."

BUT SERIOUSLY, COACH . . .

When Darryl Dawkins was an undisciplined young player with the Philadelphia 76ers in 1978, Coach Billy Cunningham was determined to make him less fun-loving and more serious.

During a practice session, the coach noticed Dawkins was goofing off and loafing on some drills. So Cunningham pulled Dawkins off the court and read him the riot act on the sidelines. The coach warned him that if he didn't shape up, he would jeopardize an otherwise promising career.

Dawkins hung his head low and said, "You're right, Coach. From now on I'm going to work hard all the time and I'll take practice much more seriously."

Cunningham, pleased that his message had finally sunk in, turned to walk back onto the court. Just then, Dawkins stuck out his foot and tripped him up. Everyone broke out laughing—including Cunningham.

CHARLES BARKLEY
Forward ○ Philadelphia 76ers ○ Jan. 6, 1987

For one game, Charles Barkley turned into a major head case. He attempted three slam dunks and all three were blocked—by his own head!

During the Philadelphia 76ers' 111–85 loss to the Los Angeles Lakers in the Forum in 1987, Barkley was hooted and scoffed at by fans when he blew a trio of monster jams. Each time, he insisted that the ball went into the basket, hit his head, and bounced back out again. But the refs refused to count the six points Barkley claimed he had made.

The all-star forward proved he was headstrong in more ways than one on his first dunk attempt of the game. After getting a lob pass directly underneath the basket, he thrust the ball with such force that it jammed through the net, bounced off his head, and came back up through the hoop. To everyone in the arena, it looked like Barkley simply blew the dunk. He argued with the refs that the basket should count, but he couldn't make any headway with them.

When the exact same thing happened a second time, Barkley was beside himself. No one would believe that the ball had gone in the basket, ricocheted off his head, and flown back out. All he got for his pleadings were snickers from the Lakers.

He almost lost his head—in more ways than one—on his third stuff of the game. After stealing the ball, Barkley went for a breakaway slam dunk. None of the Lakers was in position to stop him, so Barkley jumped high for a monster reverse jam. Incredibly, the ball bounced out once again and the refs signaled no basket.

Barkley threw his hands up in despair and pointed to his head. With his face contorted in a mixture of anger, surprise, and frustration, he argued in vain with the refs.

The proof he needed didn't surface until the day after the game. Freelance photographer Steve Dykes found the evidence on film that Barkley had made at least the third dunk before his head had knocked the ball back up through the basket.

Dykes had caught Barkley going up for the flashy, rim-rattling, two-handed backward dunk. "I was courtside shooting pictures," Dykes recalled. "When I processed the film the next day, it clearly showed Barkley with his head up inside the net, his hands on the rim, and the ball down inside the basket. The only way it could have come back out was if it bounced off his head.

Steve Dykes

"Barkley had been arguing that he missed three dunks the same way, but no one believed him. He was swearing up and down it was true, but the Lakers just laughed at him and the refs wouldn't even listen."

When Barkley learned of the photo (shown here), he said smugly, "I knew that the ball hit my head and came back out. Now I've got the proof I was right. But what ticks me off is that the refs still didn't give me those baskets."

CHARLES "HELICOPTER" HENTZ

Forward ○ Pittsburgh Condors ○ Nov. 6, 1970

Helicopter Hentz set the American Basketball Association record in backboard-busting dunks by demolishing not one but two backboards in one game.

His second slam brought the crowd to its feet—and an end to the game because the home team ran out of backboards.

Hentz, a 6-foot, 6-inch, 225-pound rookie, earned the nickname Helicopter for his leaping ability and astonishing hang time. But the Carolina Cougars remembered him as the Destroyer after he single-handedly wiped out their entire supply of glass backboards.

Hentz got the first board during the second quarter of the game at the Dorton Arena in Raleigh, North Carolina. He took a pass on a fast break, cut in from the side, and went high for the easy dunk. But his forearm hit the rim, and the laminated glass and plastic backboard shattered into a million pieces.

Basketball Hall of Fame

The rim came crashing down as Hentz and several Carolina cheerleaders sitting under the basket were showered with shrapnel. Fortunately, no one was seriously injured.

The referees halted the game while Carolina officials went in search of a new backboard. The only thing they could find was an antique wooden board gathering dust in a storage shed. Maintenance men spent an hour taking down the remnants of the glass board and installing the replacement.

They wasted their time, because late in the second half Helicopter Hentz went flying on another seek and destroy mission. "I stole the ball at midcourt and went in for the lay-up all alone," Hentz recalled. "As I was going downcourt, all I could hear was the crowd chanting, 'Tear it down! Tear it down!'

"I really didn't mean to, but when I hit the dunk, damned if that board didn't explode in my face just like the first one. Boom! I thought a bomb had gone off. I'd never even heard of someone breaking a board before, so I figured the first time was just a freak. But then I went and did it again. I couldn't believe it."

Condor coach Jack McMahon couldn't believe it either. "When Hentz was going in on the second breakaway, I thought to myself, 'Oh, no! Don't do it.' But he did it," McMahon later recalled. "We were down by 15 points and since there was only about a minute left to play, I conceded the game. We had to. There weren't any more backboards."

The Condors lost the game 122–107, but the Cougars lost their backboards.

"The thing that upset me more than losing was that those people tried to make me pay for the backboards," said Hentz. "They sent me a bill for $750.

"I told them to stuff it."

ZEBRA ZEROES

Referees are part of the game, like air balls, turnovers, and losing streaks. Without them, what would fans have to complain about? Grudgingly, fans must admit that referees are pretty honest fellows. It's just that the men in the striped shirts aren't always right. They sometimes miss calls that can be spotted by the fans in the last row of the upper tier. For "The Most Flagrantly Blown Calls by Referees," The Basketball Hall of SHAME inducts the following:

STAN STUTZ   SID BORGIA

April 12, 1952

Ten thousand spectators in St. Paul Auditorium saw forward Al McGuire sink a basket for the New York Knicks during the first game of the 1952 NBA Finals.

New York coach Joe Lapchick and the rest of the Knicks saw the ball go through the hoop.

So did the rival Minneapolis Lakers.

So did Maurice Podoloff, president of the NBA, and Pat Kennedy, the man in charge of the NBA's referee corps.

Unbelievably, the only ones who missed seeing the goal were the referees on the floor, Stan Stutz and Sid Borgia!

And since both officials didn't see McGuire's shot go in, they refused to count it.

The blown call was one of the most critical officiating gaffes in NBA history. It directly affected the outcome of the entire championship series.

Late in the first period, New York's McGuire drove for the basket and was fouled by Lakers guard Pep Saul just as the Knicks forward got off the shot. The ball swished through the net. When Borgia whistled for a two-shot foul, the players reminded him that McGuire had made the basket. But after conferring with his officiating partner,

Borgia refused to allow the field goal that everybody else in the arena had seen.

"We didn't see it go in," explained Borgia, "so we can't count it."

Borgia's decision ignited Coach Lapchick and the entire Knicks team. The New York coach stormed up and down the sideline. The two officials were not swayed by Lapchick's protest that their sudden attack of blindness was costing the Knicks at least one and possibly two points.

Podoloff and Kennedy, attending the game as spectators, were dragged into the courtside rhubarb that interrupted the game for several minutes. Finally, after Lapchick announced he would file a formal protest over the call, the game continued with the Lakers leading 19–13.

Borgia awarded McGuire two free throws since he was fouled in the act of shooting. McGuire made only one of the charity tosses.

The refs' blunder later haunted the Knicks when they fought back and tied the game at 71–71 in regulation time. But they couldn't keep up with the Lakers in overtime as Jim Pollard scored seven of his game-high 34 points and led Minneapolis to an 83–79 win.

When the series moved to New York, Podoloff held a formal hearing to consider Lapchick's protest. But Podoloff backed the referees' claim that they didn't see McGuire make the basket and the protest was disallowed.

Had the Knicks not been cheated out of at least one and possibly two points, they probably would have beaten the Lakers in regulation time. But Minneapolis' overtime victory gave the Lakers the one-game edge they needed to eventually take the best of seven championship series, four games to three.

FRANK LANE

Feb. 20, 1932

The University of Kentucky lost a game because a confused referee called a foul on a Wildcat player for accidentally hacking his own teammate!

But rather than admit he had blown an inadvertent whistle, the official awarded Vanderbilt the free throw. Vandy made the gift shot, which proved to be the margin of victory.

Interestingly, the befuddled referee went on to become one of major league baseball's most respected general managers—Frank

Lane, who was GM for the Chicago White Sox, Cleveland Indians, St. Louis Cardinals, and Milwaukee Brewers.

Long before he made his mark in baseball, Lane was a referee in the Southeastern Conference, where he often officiated games involving the Kentucky Wildcats. In 1932, Kentucky was riding a 15-game winning streak when it took on the Vanderbilt Commodores.

The teams played tough defense and traded shot for shot, with neither side able to build any kind of a lead. Midway in the second half with the score tied, a Kentucky shot bounced off the rim. Wildcats center Aggie Sale grabbed the rebound and went up for the follow-up shot when Lane blew his whistle.

The ref called a two-shot foul on Kentucky's Dutch Kreuter for hacking Sale's arms. Sale didn't question the logic of the mixed-up official and raced to the line to shoot his two freebies.

But before Sale could take the shot, Vandy's captain suddenly howled in protest. "Wait a minute," he demanded. Turning to Lane, he said, "Who committed the foul?"

Lane casually pointed at Kreuter—and then did a double take when he realized that the offender was in a Kentucky uniform. The young ref knew he couldn't call one Wildcat for fouling another Wildcat. Lane was so flustered and embarrassed that it didn't dawn on him to admit his mistake, ignore the "foul," and get on with the game. Instead, he compounded the problem.

Reversing himself, the blushing official marched the teams to the other end of the court and, for some unknown reason, awarded one free throw to *Vanderbilt!* The Commodores made the shot and won the game by a single point: 32–31.

FOR THE MAN WHO HAS EVERYTHING

During a 1938 game at Kentucky, University of Pittsburgh coach Doc Carlson was convinced the referees were "homers" favoring the Wildcats.

Midway through the second half, Carlson could no longer contain himself after another call went against his squad. He gathered up his team's sweat suits, towels, and practice balls. Then he walked over to the Kentucky bench and plopped the equipment at the feet of Coach Adolph Rupp.

"Those officials are giving you everything," Carlson told the surprised Rupp. "You might as well take these, too!"

JACK MADDEN   MIKE MATHIS

May 13, 1987

In one of the most blatant oversights in NBA playoff history, the referees failed to see that Atlanta Hawks star Dominique Wilkins had leaped into the crowd while trying to save an errant pass. As a result, the refs allowed the Detroit Pistons to inbound the ball and score while the Hawks were a man short.

It was the pivotal play of the game. The refs' blunder paved the way for the Pistons, who were losing in the final minutes of a 1987 Eastern Conference semifinal contest, to pull out the victory.

The Central Division champion Hawks were leading 93–90 with 3:05 left in the game when Wilkins tried desperately to save a wild pass that sailed toward the Atlanta bench. He went flying out of bounds and soared over two courtside tables crowded with reporters and officials. His momentum left him sprawled in the second row of spectator seats. As Atlanta's Omni crowd cheered Wilkins for his valiant effort, he tried to untangle himself from the legs and chairs of the fans.

But, incredibly, referees Jack Madden and Mike Mathis somehow failed to notice the flight and crash landing of Atlanta's 6-foot, 8-inch, 200-pound Human Highlight Film. While Wilkins was still trapped behind the press tables, the refs whistled for play to resume.

Atlanta coach Mike Fratello gestured wildly that the Hawks were missing a man, but the refs ignored the tumult from the Atlanta bench. Willing to take full advantage of the officials' bungle, Pistons guard Isiah Thomas quickly grabbed the ball from Madden's hands and put it in play. He fired a pass to teammate Rick Mahorn, who scored easily on the five-man-to-four mismatch, slicing Atlanta's lead to 93–92.

A howling Fratello called time-out and raged at Madden and Mathis for allowing Detroit such an unfair advantage. He punctuated his protest by kicking the scorer's table—and picked up a technical foul along with a sore toe. Amid the bedlam and outrage of the fans, Thomas walked to the free throw line and calmly sank the tying point. The stunned Hawks never recovered. Detroit breezed to a 104–96 victory and wrapped up the Eastern Division playoffs four games to one.

"That play really turned around a lot of things," Mahorn said after the game. "The momentum changed."

In the losers' locker room, a disgusted Wilkins fumed, "About

16,000 other people in the Omni saw me leap into the stands. How come two officials couldn't?"

BOB RAKEL

Nov. 6, 1969

In an incredible blunder, referee Bob Rakel disallowed a game-tying basket because he claimed it came after the buzzer—even though the buzzer hadn't sounded yet because there was still one second left on the clock!

Despite irrefutable evidence to the contrary, Rakel refused to change his ruling, giving the Atlanta Hawks a 124–122 win over the Chicago Bulls. His hardheaded decision infuriated the Bulls, who then filed a protest with the league office. The commissioner was so embarrassed by Rakel's gaffe that he sided with the Bulls in the only protest ever upheld by the NBA.

Trailing by two points in the final seconds at the Chicago Stadium, the Bulls tried a desperation shot that bounced off the rim. But Chicago center Tom Boerwinkle tipped it in to tie the game.

However, Rakel stunned the jubilant Bulls when he blew his whistle and signaled the basket didn't count because he said he heard the buzzer ending the game. No one in the entire stadium heard it, but Rakel's officiating partner nonetheless deferred to him.

Chicago coach Dick Motta and general manager Pat Williams were outraged. They pointed to the clock that still showed one second left to play. But Rakel wouldn't budge. Game over . . . no basket, he insisted.

Motta appealed to the timekeeper, Jim Serry, who told Rakel that he hadn't touched the clock or the buzzer and that a second definitely remained after Boerwinkle's tip-in.

"I knew it was good when it went in," recalled Boerwinkle. "Hell, there was still enough time left for lunch."

The Bulls gathered more evidence to support their case. With the press corps crowded around the scorer's table, Williams had Serry start the clock. A second passed before the buzzer sounded. Even videotaped replays showed time on the clock when the shot was made.

Rakel still refused to accept the evidence and stalked off the court. Williams then announced he was filing a formal protest and plunked down the $1,000 deposit required by the NBA.

After sorting through the evidence, Commissioner Walter Kennedy, in an unprecedented move, upheld the Bulls' protest. He ordered the game resumed with one second left on the clock, the score tied, and Atlanta in possession.

Three months later, before the Hawks' next regularly scheduled game in Chicago, the two teams played out the suspended contest. This time, the players and not a phantom buzzer heard only by the referee would decide the contest. But in an ironic twist of fate, the buzzer still managed to create controversy.

When the Hawks inbounded the ball, Boerwinkle deflected the pass and both teams scrambled for the loose ball. Atlanta's Lou Hudson came up with it, dribbled crosscourt, and then realized, as all the other players had, too, that more than just a second *had* to have passed—yet the buzzer hadn't sounded!

"In all our preparations for the replay," recalled Motta, "the clock had been set, but the buzzer hadn't! That made us look terrible."

Now it was the Hawks who howled. "See! See!" Atlanta coach Richie Guerin bellowed to the officials. "They've had weeks to work on the buzzer and it still doesn't work!"

But the officials ruled that the one second in question had expired and the game went into overtime. The Bulls lost in the extra period 142–137 but won a moral victory because their protest had been upheld. They had proved that referee Bob Rakel had been hearing things.

THE BOTTOM
OF THE BARREL

Basketball has endured many shameful blemishes that the purists would just as soon forget. The sport has been blighted by horrendous routs, boring stalls, wild brawls, and woeful teams. Fortunately, these travesties are few and far between. For "The Most Ignoble Debacles," The Basketball Hall of SHAME inducts the following:

MINNEAPOLIS LAKERS vs.
FT. WAYNE PISTONS

Nov. 22, 1950

It was the most boring game in NBA history.

The Ft. Wayne Pistons, hitting on only one cylinder, and the Minneapolis Lakers, totally frozen over, played a 48-minute stall while the crowd booed and jeered.

The Pistons won by the incredibly low score of 19–18.

The game was billed as a 50-cent father-son night promotion and the stands at the Minneapolis Auditorium were packed with proud dads eager to expose their wide-eyed sons to the excitement of high-octane pro basketball. But before the first half ended, the less-than-impressed youngsters in the balcony were bored. And thousands of ticked-off fans were demanding their money back.

Ft. Wayne coach Murray Mendenhall concocted the shameful scheme as a desperate attempt to beat the two-time defending champion Lakers, who were sporting a home-court winning streak of 29 straight victories.

The Pistons stalled from the opening tip-off. Ft. Wayne controlled the tip, but when the Lakers set up their defense and turned around, they were surprised to see Pistons center Larry Foust standing near midcourt, holding the ball on his hip. The Lakers waited for the Pistons to move, but Foust, under strict orders from Mendenhall, stayed planted. The plan was to force the Lakers to come out in a man-to-man defense.

With neither side willing to move, the first quarter turned into a long, dull standoff interrupted by an occasional pass. While the Lakers taunted the Pistons to play basketball, many of the 7,021 fans booed and stamped their feet in disgust. But the Ft. Wayne players stuck to their do-nothing game plan.

Occasionally, exasperated Minneapolis guard Slater Martin would harass the ball handler and force a turnover. When he was successful, the Lakers would pass the ball to their star scorer, center George Mikan. (Mikan wound up scoring 15 of the Lakers' 18 points, including all of the team's four field goals.)

At the end of the first quarter, the Pistons led 8–7. If the fans were hoping for more scoring, they were sorely disappointed. Those would be the most points scored in any of the periods.

The game kept up its Rip Van Winkle pace with the yawning Lakers watching the yawning Pistons hold the ball for three or four minutes at a stretch. The stall unnerved the Lakers, who, on the rare times they got possession of the ball, twice blew easy lay-ups. With Ft. Wayne failing to attempt a single shot from the floor, Minneapolis captured the lead at the break, 13–11.

When the second half resumed, the Lakers were content to sit on the lead as long as the Pistons were content to sit on the ball.

"During the game, the fans were leaving," recalled Slater Martin. "They wanted their money back. It was boring to watch a team sitting on the ball. It got so bad, people were reading newspapers in the stands. They had to do something."

Minneapolis entered the fourth quarter ahead 17–16. With about six minutes left in the game, the Lakers' Jim Pollard sank a free throw—which turned out to be the team's only point of the entire period.

Trailing 18–17 with nine seconds left on the clock, Ft. Wayne made its move. Curly Armstrong fed the ball to a breaking Larry Foust, who managed to sink an off-balance hook shot over Mikan's outstretched arms. The Lakers rushed downcourt, but Martin's last-second desperation shot bounced off the rim and the lowest-scoring, most boring game in NBA history mercifully ended.

John Kundla, the disgusted Lakers' coach, fumed, "If that's basketball, I don't want any part of it. They'll kill pro basketball playing that kind of game."

But Mendenhall was elated after the victory and defended his tactics. "Why should we knock our heads against a stone wall?" he said. "Trying to work the ball in against the Lakers is impossible, so we played to pull them out. If they didn't come out, that's not our fault. We had the ball. It was their job to come and get it."

The debacle set a record for the most "leasts" ever recorded in an NBA game. Among them were:

- Least points for a team—18. (The previous record low was 38.)
- Least points by two teams—37. (The previous record low was 83.)
- Least field goals by a team—4, shared by the Lakers and the Pistons. (The previous record was 13.)
- Least attempted shots per game—13, Pistons. (No previous record was kept.)
- Least attempted shots per quarter—0, Pistons. (No previous record was kept.)
- Least points per quarter—1, Lakers. (No previous record was kept.)

Minneapolis sportswriter Charles Johnson called the game a "sports tragedy." About the only good to come from it was that the league was eventually motivated to adopt the 24-second rule and eliminate the zone defense.

After the game, angry league president Maurice Podoloff snapped, "I don't want anything like that to ever happen again." Fortunately, for fans and players alike, it hasn't.

ENGLEWOOD CLIFFS COLLEGE

Jan. 20, 1974

No team ever suffered a more devastating, more overwhelming defeat than Englewood Cliffs College. The small New Jersey junior college was crushed 210–67.

Following the lopsided lambasting, Englewood not only gave up basketball but also locked its doors and went entirely belly-up.

The 143-point deficit was the worst shellacking in collegiate history. But don't blame it on poor defense; it was more like poor scheduling. The eroding Cliffs had to play the intrastate powerhouse Essex County Community College Wolverines, whose offense had been racking up bowling scores all season long. By the time the two teams met at the crackerbox YMCA gym in Newark, the 17–3 Wolverines had lit up scoreboards with such tallies as 160, 141, 139, 132, and 130 points. Englewood Cliffs was lucky to score that many points in a week.

The outmanned and outgunned Cliffs knew they were in for a long night when Wolverines guard Stanley Williams hit the first six points of the game off steals alone. Before Englewood could even find the basket, Essex had roared to a 26–0 lead—and the game was hardly four minutes old.

Harassed by a full-court press, the woebegone Cliffs changed their objectives. Instead of trying to score, they just tried to get the ball over the center stripe. In the rare instances when they actually took a shot, their attempts were often swatted back like flies. The Wolverines swept the boards clean—they garnered an incredible 89 rebounds—and ran the fast break like convicts on the loose. Six-foot, 6-inch center Arthur Pope pulled down 28 boards himself and blocked 11 shots.

The Cliffs gave up their first 100 points before the half was even over. Then beleaguered coach Ed Salkiewicz began arguing that Pope should be called for goaltending—as if it really mattered. Salkiewicz protested so loudly that he kept drawing technical fouls. When he refused to sit down and shut up, the coach was thrown out of the game. Essex promptly scored another five points off Salkiewicz's "T's."

"I don't know what his problem was," recalled Essex coach Cleo Hill. "It was like trying to plug the hole in the dike after the dam had busted."

At halftime, the Cliffs trailed by *only* 81 points, 110–29. Meanwhile, the Essex players learned from a radio announcer that they were within reach of breaking the single-game collegiate scoring record of 202 points.

"I really didn't want to embarrass Englewood," Coach Hill said. "But the kids asked me to let them have a shot at the record and I said OK."

The Wolverines came out running and gunning in the second half. "We'd clear the boards and have three or four guys out on the break before Englewood even knew we had the ball," said Hill. "Also, I kept changing the defense and that really confused them. We'd score, steal the ball, and score again a couple of times before they could get past halfcourt."

With three minutes left to play, the Wolverines called time-out. They were still 21 points shy of the record. The Cliffs were still shy of the ball. When play resumed, Englewood Cliffs turned the ball over a dozen times as Essex scored 29 more points before the final buzzer mercifully sounded. The Wolverines owned the scoring record . . . and the Cliffs owned the blowout record.

For the game, Essex shot an astonishing 97 for 129 from the floor, a shooting percentage of 75 percent. "That old scoreboard looked like an adding machine trying to keep up with us," recalled Hill. "I was afraid it wasn't going to make it."

Later, the game ball and the page from the scorebook made it to the Basketball Hall of Fame.

The saga of Englewood Cliffs, meanwhile, made it to The Basketball Hall of SHAME.

WOOD YOU MIND TAKING IT EASIER ON ME!

During a rough game with the Philadelphia 76ers in 1987, Los Angeles Lakers forward Kurt Rambis was kicked in the head,

Andrew D. Bernstein/NBA Photos

knocked to the floor, and shoved out of bounds—all in the span of 20 seconds.

"I was just getting acquainted with the wood," he said after the game. "I wanted to see if it was pine or maple."

ALABAMA CRIMSON TIDE vs. KENTUCKY WILDCATS

Feb. 28, 1955

In one of the most outrageous pregame confrontations in college basketball history, players from Alabama and Kentucky stood eyeball to eyeball at midcourt and tried to outstare each other.

Then somebody blinked. In a flash, challenges were hurled, the line was crossed, and fists were thrown. Suddenly players, coaches, spectators, cops, and even reporters tangled in a wild melee on the floor.

It all began over a pregame ritual practiced by the Kentucky Wildcats. Before home games, Kentucky coach Adolph Rupp liked to send his second stringers out to midcourt. There they stared daggers at the opposing team during warm-ups and made snide comments that only the visitors could hear. Such insults as, "Hey, dummy. You couldn't guard your jockstrap" were intended to distract and intimidate, which they usually did, since Kentucky rarely lost under Rupp.

But when Alabama coach Johnny Dee and his Crimson Tide arrived at Lexington to battle for the 1954–55 Southeastern Conference title and a postseason tournament berth, the visitors were ready to stare back.

"If Rupp had 12 guys warming up, half of them would go and stand at halfcourt and stare your kids down to intimidate them when they were taking lay-ups," Dee recalled.

"I always thought it was a bush league thing for Kentucky to send guys out there to gawk and make comments. I figured the best way to beat them at their own game was to have our kids stare right back."

As soon as the Wildcats' reserves lined up at center court and started staring, Dee sent his own subs out to fight glare with glare. Kentucky stood on one side of the center line with Alabama on the other side only inches apart.

The stare-down continued for several minutes until Alabama's

6-foot, 7-inch center Jim Bogan drew an imaginary line on the floor with his toe and dared Kentucky's 5-foot, 11-inch guard Don Chandler to cross over.

"Bogan called me a yellow so-and-so because I wouldn't cross the line," recalled Chandler. "I told him he was going to get one drubbing tonight and better not be looking for another one. That's when I walked across his line. He started swinging, hitting me on the chin. Then I cut loose."

Bogan offered a slightly different version of what happened: "They didn't like it when we stared back at them. Chandler cussed me out. Then he came at me and swung. I swung back."

The sudden breakdown in stare diplomacy triggered an explosive free-for-all. As soon as Chandler and Bogan started punching, the substitutes at midcourt leaped on one another. Spectators and reporters poured out of the stands to join in. Then local cops and state troopers jumped into the growing pile of bodies to restore order.

While Rupp and Dee were willing to sacrifice their subs, both coaches remained on the sideline and kept their starting lineups safely out of the fray. "We were all trying to get in," recalled 'Bama guard Leon Marlaire. "But Coach Dee had all the starters on the bench, and he was saying, 'You can't get in! You just sit here!' It was the biggest brawl I've ever seen."

At one point, Bogan was pinned to the floor while a Wildcat gnawed on his chest. "It's kind of weird lying there with your arms pinned down while a guy bites on you, and you're watching him do it," said Bogan.

After order was restored, the game began. Surprisingly, the teams played cleanly, and Kentucky won 66–52.

Following the game, Dee shrugged off the confrontation.

"I just sent my subs out to halfcourt to stare back at the other side," he explained. "One of my kids drew an imaginary line and dared Kentucky to cross it. They did and we had a little scuffle. Actually, I guess it was more than a little scuffle since the Kentucky state troopers came out in force to break it up."

Wildcats partisans later accused Dee of deliberately instigating the brawl by offering a bounty to any of his subs who could get a Kentucky player to cross the line during the stare-down. "No comment," said Dee of the charge. "But I noticed that after the fight, Kentucky dropped the practice of staring at people."

LOS ANGELES CLIPPERS

1986–87

During the 1980s in Los Angeles, serious fans of basketball went to see the Lakers. People who thought basketball was a joke watched the Clippers.

They both got their money's worth.

The L.A. Clippers—aka the Coupon Clippers—owned the NBA's comedy corner throughout the decade, even before they were transplanted in 1984 from San Diego, where they were sometimes called the Flippers (because they played their games near Sea World).

Not only did the Clippers never have a winning season during the entire dismal decade but they were so inept that they averaged an astounding 57 losses per year.

The team's disgrace peaked during the 1986–87 season when they finished with a 12–70 record, the second worst in NBA history. They capped the year in characteristic style by losing their last 19 games—14 of them at home in front of the handful of ticket holders who wandered into the arena in the mistaken belief that the other L.A. team was playing.

Coach Don Chaney, who not surprisingly was fired at the end of the season, called his time spent with the Clippers "a nightmare." Said Chaney, "We were almost afraid to play each game. I couldn't sleep. . . . Everything that could go bad did."

In fact, for three straight seasons—1986 through 1988—the Clippers couldn't even win a measly 20 games. They didn't quite match the woeful 9–73 mark set by the 1972–73 Philadelphia 76ers—the worst won-lost record in NBA history. But they tried. They surpassed the Sixers' dubious distinction as the only pro team to lose in 22 American cities. (The Sixers did it at a time when there were only 17 teams in the league and some games were played at neutral sites.) Midway through the 1986–87 season, long after the NBA had expanded, the Clippers lost in all 23 league cities.

"I replayed every loss in my head," recalled Chaney. "It was embarrassing. I didn't like walking out of an arena and having people laugh at us. It was tough for me to sleep at night. I got migraine headaches and I'd never had them before. The season was an example of Murphy's Law at work."

Unfortunately, Murphy's Law went into effect before the season even opened. The team lost most of its key players to either injury or disgust. For example, Derek Smith, the team's top scorer the two

previous seasons, simply refused to be seen in public in a Clippers uniform any longer and was traded. Meanwhile, former Laker Norm Nixon, whom the Clippers were counting on as the team leader, ruptured his Achilles tendon playing softball and was of no use.

Ex-Bull Quintin Dailey, who was best known in Chicago for snacking on pizza on the bench during a game, joined the Clippers 25 pounds overweight—and was suspended for being too fat.

All-star Marques Johnson, acquired from Milwaukee, was hailed as a possible savior. But during an early-season game against the Dallas Mavericks, Johnson grabbed a rebound, turned upcourt, and ran head-on into the large belly of a teammate, center Benoit Benjamin. Big Ben didn't budge. Johnson suffered a career-ending neck injury.

For Chaney, the loss of Johnson was one more cross to bear. "Without Marques, we were a leaderless team," sighed Chaney. "I'll bet we lost 15 games in the fourth quarter because nobody wanted the ball."

Benjamin (shown on the floor in photo) may have been the perfect Clipper. This was the guy who once arrived for a game with two left shoes. Benjamin also was one of the team's tubbies. Overweight by 27 pounds or more, Benjamin waddled up and down the court in such obvious distress that the trainer had to swab down his thighs with Vaseline to ease the chafing.

"If Benoit hadn't eaten in two days and he was thrown into a cage with a grizzly bear, you can rest assured somebody would come out wearing a fur coat," said teammate Cedric Maxwell.

Before the 1986–87 season opened, the Clippers took out an ad in the Los Angeles papers brazenly predicting they would win the NBA title. The only title they earned was to the cellar. They posted an embarrassing 17–65 record and finished 53 games behind the Pacific Division winners—their classy neighbors, the Lakers.

Each of those 65 losses was a textbook example of how not to play basketball. A game against the Milwaukee Bucks was typical of the Clippers' pitiful performance. Los Angeles was battling tough and trailed by only four points in the closing minutes when Clippers forward Rory White went in for an uncontested lay-up. He tried a showboating dunk. But the ball bounced off the rim all the way to midcourt, where the Bucks got the long-distance rebound, scored, and then cruised to a 110–100 win.

In another game, Phoenix Suns forward Eddie Johnson proved that the Clippers' defense had taken the night off. He scored 33 points against L.A.—all in the first half.

The Clippers became the NBA's laughingstock because management made some of the most creative trading blunders in league history. They used their number one draft picks to grab such future all-stars as Byron Scott, Tom Chambers, and Terry Cummings—and let them all slip away. (Their number one pick in 1989, Danny Ferry, didn't even bother to negotiate with them but opted for the obscurity of Italian basketball rather than play for the Clippers.)

"We collected guys off the streets to play for us," moaned Chaney. "Sometimes I looked out on the floor at all those no-names and I couldn't believe my eyes."

Guard Darnell Valentine put it another way: "When you play for the Clippers, you feel like you're coming over on one of those boats from Cuba with all different kinds of people on it."

The Clippers' collective inferiority complex wasn't helped any by the attitude of the front office. Owner Donald Sterling once indicated that as long as the team was losing, it might as well lose as many games as possible to nail down the number one draft pick. "Maybe I have to lose the battle to win the war," said Sterling. But Commissioner Larry O'Brien wasn't amused. He slam dunked Sterling with a $10,000 fine for ". . . conduct detrimental to basketball."

Ousted coach Don Chaney summed up the sad-sack season: "It was horrendous and there probably won't be another like it for a long time."

Fans everywhere hope he's right.

TENNESSEE TECH GOLDEN EAGLES vs. MOREHEAD STATE EAGLES

Jan. 6, 1951

A broken game clock turned the clash between Tennessee Tech and Morehead State into a ridiculous farce with twice the playing time of a regular game.

The contest dragged on until Tech's Golden Eagles and State's Eagles were worn to a frazzle. So many players fouled out in the drawn-out game that Morehead State wound up with only three men on the court.

And that's when it turned into a real debacle.

After most of his team had fouled out, Morehead State coach Ellis Johnson threw off his coat and shucked his shoes—and played the few remaining minutes himself!

Because Tennessee Tech's basketball court was being repaired, the 1951 game was played in the old gym at the local high school in Cookeville, Tennessee. By the end of the first half, it was obvious that the game clock was so slow it couldn't even pass the time of day. An hourglass would have been more accurate. The puzzled referees suspected something was wrong with the official timepiece but decided the second half should be played under the same conditions as the first half.

So the game went on . . . and on . . . and on. The longer the teams played, the more they fouled. The refs were blowing whistles like overworked traffic cops and called a total of 77 fouls. Player after player began fouling out. Meanwhile, the survivors were so tired that they ran at half-speed, which was still faster than the clock was moving.

"We didn't think we were ever going to get out of there," recalled Flavius Smith, the Tech center. "We played what amounted to almost two full games, but the officials wouldn't let us quit until that old clock said the game was over. Everybody who hadn't fouled out by that time was totally exhausted."

And while the game dragged on in slow motion, Johnson grew more and more irritated with the fiasco.

"He kept trying to tell the referees something was wrong with the clock, but they ignored him," recalled Don Miller, a member of the Morehead State squad.

"One time we called time-out and when we went over to the bench, Coach Johnson was gone. We found him sitting about 10 rows up in the stands eating popcorn with some students. He'd just gotten bored with the whole thing and was trying to show what a mockery the game was."

Twelve players eventually fouled out. With the clock creeping through the final couple of minutes, the seventh Morehead State player was whistled to the bench, leaving only three teammates on the floor.

That's when Coach Johnson got into the act. He whipped off his coat, kicked off his shoes, and ran to the scorers' table to check in.

"Of course, they wouldn't let him in—officially," said Smith. "But he went in and played anyway. It was a big joke. We were staggering around in exhaustion and here was the other team's coach out there slipping and sliding around in his stocking feet."

The only points Johnson scored were with the fans, who laughed themselves silly at the coach's antics. After what seemed like an eternity, the final buzzer sounded. The game ended with Tech winning 90–88, and this during an era when scoring 50 points was a remarkable achievement.

Later in the season, when Tech traveled to Morehead, Kentucky, for a rematch, an elaborate pregame ceremony was staged in which Johnson presented his rival coach with a big brass alarm clock—one that worked.

Recalling the untimely game, Johnson told reporters, "You know what bothered me the most about that game? My own players wouldn't pass the ball to me."

RHODE ISLAND RAMS vs.
MAINE BLACK BEARS

Feb. 22, 1948

In one of the most shameful travesties ever seen on a college basketball court, the Rhode Island Rams outvaudevilled the Maine Black Bears.

The 3,200 fans who came to see some hoops wound up watching basketball burlesque. On the floor during the game, Maine players acted like statues while their Rhode Island counterparts did a lousy impersonation of the Harlem Globetrotters. For a finale, a Ram played his harmonica and another punted the ball into the rafters. Through it all, their teammates read comic books.

The fans at Maine's Alumni Gymnasium rated the wacky performance with thumbs down—and a raining down of popcorn, bottles, and other trash.

The debacle was triggered by the Black Bears' attempt to slow down the hot-shooting Rams, who were scorching the nets with 100-point games at a time when scoring that many points was as rare as swishing a shot from the opposite end of the court.

"Maine figured the only way they could stay with us was to play a slow-down game," recalled Ken Goodwin, the Rhode Island center.

"A Maine player told me they didn't expect to win. They considered it a moral victory if they could keep us from scoring 100 points.

"In the game, we'd back off and let them go in for a lay-up just so we could get the ball. But they'd dribble right out the other side and wouldn't even shoot an uncontested lay-up. We couldn't get them to come out and play. The referees tried, but Maine wouldn't budge. The game degenerated into a total fiasco that embarrassed both sides."

Maine jumped right into the deep freeze with the opening tip-off. The game was only a few minutes old before Rhode Island vaulted to an 11–2 lead. But the Black Bears made no attempt to win; their goal was to keep the Rams from racking up a big score. The Rhode Island players, used to their run-and-gun approach, grew increasingly frustrated over the lack of action and started taunting their opponents.

Even Maine's own supporters became annoyed with the boring, four-corner game that the Black Bears played. "At first, the crowd was dumbfounded over the slow-down antics and started hooting and booing," recalled Len Harlow, who covered the game as a student reporter. "When it continued, they started throwing bottles and trash on the floor to show their displeasure."

At the end of the first half, Rhode Island led 29–17. But Rams coach Frank Keaney (shown in photo on p. 109) was so ticked off he decided to fight farce with farce.

After challenging the refs to forfeit the game, Keaney stormed over to the Maine bench and shouted to Coach George "Eck" Allen, "I'll show you a comedy to end all comedies!"

With six minutes left to play, Keaney sent in reserve Mike Santoro, who suddenly whipped out his harmonica. "When Mike checked in, the travesty really started," said Goodwin. "We passed the ball to him and he sat on it at center court and serenaded the crowd with 'Silent Night.' " But the night was hardly silent as the crowd booed louder than ever and the refs kicked Santoro out of the game.

Meanwhile, Keaney, who had arrived in Maine anticipating the stall, dug out a pile of comic books and newspapers he had brought along for the occasion. The coach passed around the reading material to his reserves on the bench.

The fans were so disgusted with both sides that they surged onto the floor. Both benches were showered with more popcorn, trash, and empty bottles.

The officials finally cleared the court and pleaded with Keaney and Allen to play straight. Both refused. When the Black Bears got the ball, they continued to hold it until fouled by a Ram. At least when the Rhode Islanders were in possession, they did something. They dribbled on their knees and passed between their legs in a poor imitation of the Harlem Globetrotters—but they wouldn't take a shot even when they had it.

"Finally," recalled Goodwin, "I was so fed up that I got the team out in the middle of the court and had them line up in a football formation. One guy centered the ball to me and I punted it as hard as I could. It rattled around up in the rafters and by the time it came back down I'd been kicked out of the game.

"I asked the ref why he was throwing me out since nobody was playing basketball anyway. He told me, 'For making a travesty of the game, since I can't get you for an illegal punt.'"

The turmoil brought Maine president Arthur Hauck out of the stands. He pleaded with Keaney to end the theatrics, but the riled coach shook his finger in Hauck's face and shouted, "Your boys conceded defeat before we even walked on the floor."

Keaney then sent most of his players to the showers and finished the game with only four Rams on the floor. They won the debacle easily, 55–43.

Had the absurdity dragged on much longer, the coach said later, "I was going to yank the whole team, take the harmonica with me, and play a tune while Maine played their silly game.

"They wanted to play slow, huh? Well, we showed 'em a stall that they won't forget up here for a long time!"

OF SOUND MIND AND BODY

University of Rhode Island coach Frank Keaney nearly lost his mind in a 1937 loss to Worcester Tech.

With less than a minute to play and Rhode Island hanging on to a 37–36 lead, Keaney sent in sophomore sub Bob Elliot with explicit instructions to stall. But as soon as Elliot touched the ball, he made a wild shot and missed. Tech rebounded, scored, and won the game 38–37.

Keaney was livid after the game and ripped into Elliot. The fuming-mad coach even told Elliot that he would not let him back on the team until the player passed a physical and mental test given by the college physician.

A few days later, after Keaney had forgotten his tirade, Elliot handed the coach a slip from the school's doctor declaring the player was "mentally and physically sound."

Keaney smiled and nodded. Then Elliot told him, "Now let's see if *you* can get one."

GOLDEN STATE WARRIORS

March 19, 1972

In the biggest blowout in NBA history, the Golden State Warriors staggered off the court, shameful losers by a whopping 63 points.

They were humiliated by the Los Angeles Lakers 162–99 in the widest losing margin in professional basketball history.

"Our minds were willing, but our bodies were not," lamented Al Attles, the Warriors' coach. "This just wasn't our night."

That was obvious from the opening tip-off, when the Lakers started running the road-weary Warriors up and down the court to the delight of the 17,505 partisan fans at the Forum. Golden State, playing for the fourth time in four successive nights, never got out of first gear.

"They were really weary," said Laker Keith Erickson. "They couldn't even complete a pass."

By the end of the first quarter, the Lakers had zoomed out to a fat 42–24 margin. Attles knew it was hopeless and, eschewing the fight-to-the-bitter-end mentality of most NBA coaches, pulled his starters from the game.

"There was no sense in beating a dead horse," Attles shrugged. But nobody told the Lakers the horse had expired. They kept pounding away at the Warriors and went to the locker room at halftime with a commanding 71–56 lead.

If the Warriors were struggling in the first half, they were sleepwalking through the last half. During an eight-minute stretch in the third quarter, Los Angeles guard Gail Goodrich single-handedly outscored the entire Golden State team, ripping the net for 19 points before taking a rest. The Warriors were outscored by an incredible 28 points in the period (49–21) and trailed 120–77 with another quarter yet to go.

Lakers coach Bill Sharman could barely conceal his glee over the lopsided game. "The scoreboard looked like a runaway pinball machine," he said. It would have lit up even more had he not finally benched his starters after the third quarter.

The only question left unanswered was how much more humiliation Golden State could take. Still playing in a daze, the Warriors, who shot a frigid 34 percent from the floor compared to the Lakers' blistering 61 percent, slipped behind another 20 points before the final horn sounded.

"The Lakers must have set a world record for lay-ups," said a shell-shocked Jim Barnett, whose 15 points was high for the Warriors. Every player in the Los Angeles lineup, except for a pair of unknown scrubs and an injured Keith Erickson, outscored the Warriors' high-point man.

The 63-point spread surpassed the old mark of 62 set by the New York Knicks, who were slaughtered by the Syracuse Nationals 162–100 in 1960. The Lakers' 162 points was a team record and only 11 shy of the then all-time NBA mark for a nonovertime game set by the Boston Celtics in 1959.

"That's why Sharman took us regulars out in the fourth quarter," said L.A. center Wilt Chamberlain. "He played on that Boston team and he was protecting their record."

THE TIN CAN GYM
Mississippi State • 1932–50

The best thing that could be said about the old Tin Can Gym at Mississippi State was that it beat playing outdoors in the mud—but not by much.

The Tin Can never had a more honorable name. It didn't deserve one. From the time it opened in 1932, the drafty, bitterly cold Quonset hut on the Bulldogs' campus earned its reputation as one of the worst college basketball facilities since Dr. Naismith nailed his peach basket to the wall.

There were no locker room facilities in the Tin Can, so the Mississippi State Bulldogs had to suit up in the locker room of the football stadium and then trudge half a mile to the gym.

Even at that they were better off than their opponents, who had to settle for the cramped men's bathroom of the Quonset hut as a dressing room. At halftime, the Bulldogs met with their coach behind a drape in one corner of the gym. The other team was forced to use the Can's can.

Playing in the Tin Can was often an ear-rattling, teeth-chattering experience, according to Jack Nix, who was on the first basketball squad that claimed the Quonset hut as its home court.

He recalled that gale-force winds often whipped through the loosely jointed tin sheets covering the surface of the building. They made a loud, annoying racket. But even worse were the freezing cold temperatures.

"Sometimes the wind was blowing so hard and your hands were so cold that you couldn't even feel the ball when you dribbled it," said Nix. "The only heat in the place came from a couple of old potbellied stoves at either end of the court behind the baskets. During the games, we were often distracted by the stove tenders, who would come in with an armload of wood and stoke the fires."

Even though the stoves barely kept icicles from forming on the nets, they did cut down considerably on overly aggressive action. Players on both teams were terrified of running into one of the stoves and being permanently branded.

Another hazard was the court itself, which was built about three feet above the floor of the Tin Can. Players new to the monstrosity frequently ran too close to the edge and fell off. "We were used to it," said Nix, "so we got pretty good at maneuvering the other guys around and running them right off the side of the court."

In 1938, John Mauer made his first trip to the Tin Can as coach of the Tennessee Volunteers. It was an awful experience he never forgot.

At the halftime break, his team had to fight for space in the men's room with fans who were heeding the call of nature. There, in the cramped quarters with johns flushing and fans combing their hair, Mauer tried to deliver a stirring pep talk. It was futile.

During the game (which Tennessee lost 25–24), the Vols could barely maintain possession of the ball. "They [the Bulldogs] had pumped the ball up too much and the damn thing bounced almost to the roof when our kids tried to dribble," said Mauer.

But it was Mississippi State's backboards that Mauer remembered most. "They had just painted the backboards, and the paint rubbed off on the ball," he said. "Once [Tennessee player] Wilton Putnam started to shoot an overhead shot from the corner. The ball just stuck to his hands! I was never so glad to get out of a place in my life."

EDGERTON PARK ARENA

Rochester, New York • 1948–57

The NBA's Rochester Royals—forerunners of the Sacramento Kings—played in an arena so small that players driving for a lay-up often sailed through doors behind the baskets and ended up outside in four feet of snow!

In Rochester's Edgerton Park Arena, players charging down the floor on a fast break had to be ready to stop on a dime. For those who couldn't manage the tricky maneuver, the Royals had volunteers stationed out of bounds at both ends of the court. Their job was to open a door just beneath the baskets. The overzealous players had to make a quick decision—smack head-on into the wall or take the open door.

The smart guys took the wall.

The ones who opted for the door at one end of the gym disappeared into the night, usually plowing into a snowdrift that piled up around the arena during Rochester's long, cold winters.

Those who went through the door at the opposite end of the court wound up with the concessionaires. "There were times when a fan would come late to the game and be carrying a hot dog and soda," recalled former Royal Red Holzman. "A player would drive for a lay-up and go through the doors. The fan, the player, the hot dog, and the soda would all scatter in different directions."

Whichever door they flew through, the embarrassed players—often covered with snow or mustard—had to trudge back into the gym, where a throng of amused and highly partisan Royals fans were waiting to heap abuse on them.

"On a lay-up there was no place else to go except the wall or the door," said Dolph Schayes, the great playmaker with the Syracuse Nationals. "This basket was right up against the wall. After a while, most guys learned to veer off toward the wall instead of ending up outdoors in the cold. But not every time. I think those fans in Rochester just lived to see some poor guy go busting through the door. Sooner or later, he had to come back in and they were really laying for him with hoots and hollers."

Savvy players often tried to con their opponents into crashing through the doors. One Royal in particular repeatedly got suckered by the open door trick.

Art Deutsch, a Syracuse team official, recalled how Billy "Bullet" Gabor of the Nationals, known throughout the league for his speed, loved to get the ball on a fast break and challenge the Royals' Bobby Davies in a race to the basket.

"Gabor would try that at least once a game when we were in Rochester," said Deutsch. "It's amazing how often Davies fell for it. Davies couldn't stop, but someone was stationed there to open the door while he went flying right out of the building."

Paul Seymour, Syracuse's player-coach, often watched players disappear through Edgerton's infamous doors.

"I've seen other guys hit the door and wind up out in the cold," he recalled. "They'd come back in stamping the snow off their shoes and looking pretty sheepish. That was really the highlight of playing at Rochester—suckering some defender into coming after you on a lay-up, then ducking at the last second and watching him go flying past you out the door.

"It wasn't wise to hang around when that happened. Usually the guy was so mad about landing in a snowdrift that he'd come back in swinging."

EVERY TRICK IN THE BOOK

To win at basketball, you need to learn the fundamentals of the game from skillful ball handling to strong rebounding. But to gain that extra edge that could make the difference between winning and losing, players and coaches need to learn the finer points—like how to run a fast break on the rules. Playing fair and square is not necessarily in their game plan. For "The Sneakiest Chicanery," The Basketball Hall of SHAME inducts the following:

ARNOLD "RED" AUERBACH

Coach–General Manager–President ● Boston Celtics ● 1950–present

When it came to pregame psychological warfare, Red Auerbach was a five-star general.

However, he did lose his share of battles.

Auerbach played some of his best mind games during the 1972 Eastern Conference finals, when the New York Knicks invaded the Boston Garden.

"We were given an old beat-up dressing room," recalled Knicks coach Red Holzman. "They wouldn't even let our guys use a whirlpool. It was all psychological warfare, the Celtic fun-and-games version."

The Knicks complained about the way they were treated and felt that Boston showed them a lack of respect. The vexed players fell victim to Auerbach's pregame psych-out and were drubbed 134–108.

New York won the second game at home. But when the Knicks returned to Beantown, Auerbach was waiting with his psychological guns primed and ready to fire.

The Knicks were assigned to a different dressing room at the Boston Garden that was even more dingy, cramped, and out of the way than the first one. "This dressing room is for jockeys, not basketball players," complained the Knicks' Walt Frazier, eyeing his stooped-

over, uncomfortable team-
mates. Added an irked Phil
Jackson, "It's a pain being
switched from place to place."

This time, Auerbach's ploy
backfired. The Knicks took
their anger out on the Celtics
on the floor and beat them
98–91. But Auerbach was not
ready to give up on his mind
games. After his team lost
again in New York to fall behind three games to one, Auerbach was more determined
than ever to get the edge on the
Knicks.

"When we went back to
Boston for the fifth game, we
were given a different dressing
room again," recalled Holz-

UPI/Bettmann

man. "This one was dusty and dirty. And it was like a sauna—the
temperature in there must have been 120 degrees."

When game time finally rolled around and the Knicks staggered
onto the court, the cool and refreshed Celtics used that thermostat
advantage to squeak out a 98–97 win.

For game six at Madison Square Garden, Auerbach had his team
wait until the Knicks started warming up and then demanded that
Boston use their basket. As the visiting team, Boston's request had to
be honored, according to NBA rules. Being forced to move to the
other side of the court irritated the New York players. With their
concentration slightly jarred, the Knicks lost, setting up the seventh
and final game back at the Boston Garden.

Auerbach resorted to the old turn-up-the-heat-in-the-locker-room
trick for the finale. But all it did was make the Knicks boiling mad.
They scalded the Celtics 94–78 to capture the conference title.

That wasn't the only time Auerbach's psychological ploys backfired. He got too carried away for his own good minutes before the
Celtics were set to play the Hawks in St. Louis in the third game of the
1957 NBA Finals

Just before tip-off time, Auerbach complained about the weight of
the basketball and insisted that it be tested. This was a variation of a
favorite Auerbach gimmick. He liked to create a diversion just seconds

before the referee threw up the jump ball to start the game. As coach of the visiting team, Auerbach invoked his right to pick the game ball. The Celtics were prepared for the interruption, but the ploy often threw the other team off its timing.

Once the ball controversy was settled, Auerbach stirred things up some more, recalled the Celtics' Jim Loscutoff. "He went to Ben Kerner, the owner of the Hawks, and bitched that the basket at one end was too low. Kerner said it was OK, but Auerbach argued that it was about one inch too low and since the Celtics would be shooting at that basket in the first half, he wanted it measured."

Finally, an exasperated Maurice Podoloff, president of the NBA, ordered a measurement to satisfy Auerbach. While maintenance workers brought out a ladder and tape measure, Auerbach and Kerner heatedly exchanged words.

"The next thing we knew, Red wound up and punched Kerner in the nose," said Loscutoff. "They had a pretty good fracas going there for a couple of minutes. We all thought it was pretty funny, watching a coach and an owner duke it out.

"It turned out that the basket was the right height anyway, but Red was so out of sorts over his fight with Kerner that he wasn't worth a damn the rest of the game. We ended up losing by two points."

More than once Auerbach has been accused of arranging to have the fire alarms set off at the hotel of an opposing team. The Los Angeles Lakers were victims of bed-rousting alarms ten times in Boston during the 1984 playoffs.

In his autobiography, *Kareem,* Kareem Abdul-Jabbar wrote, "In Boston, the hotel alarms began waking us up on the Saturday night before Game 1 and continued waking us up nightly until Thursday when we played Game 2. There wasn't a doubt in my mind or in the team's mind that the alarms had been intentionally triggered to disrupt our sleep."

No one could prove Auerbach was behind the distraction, but he was accused of it anyway. Said Celtics great Bob Cousy, "If room service is slow, or there is a fire alarm in the hotel at three in the morning, or even if it rains, there are people in the NBA who believe to this day that Auerbach is behind it. Everything remotely nefarious is attributed to Red. Other people would be offended. Auerbach just takes another puff [on his cigar] and smiles."

LARKIN RUCKER

Coach • Bluefield State Big Blues • Dec. 14, 1963

Like a sneaky politician, Bluefield State coach Larkin Rucker used some unfair lobbying tactics to steal a win.

In the closing minutes of an overtime game with the visiting Beckley College Blue Hawks, the Bluefield coach ordered the Big Blues to run his secret "sleeper" play. The scheme called for Bluefield guard Don McDowell to step out into the lobby of the Big Blues' gym for a drink of water while his four teammates took the floor. Then he would pop back in under his own basket, catch a long pass from the other end of the court, and score an uncontested lay-up.

With the Blue Hawks at the opposite end of the court, there was no one to guard the lone McDowell. The Big Blues successfully pulled off the play twice before Beckley coach Joe Cook caught on to the deception.

By then it was too late. The four points were just enough for Bluefield to outlast Beckley 90–86.

"They may have called it the sleeper play," recalled Cook. "To me it was unfair lobbying on their part."

The play was designed around a door under one basket in the small West Virginia gymnasium that opened to a lobby. During time-outs, players frequently dashed out to the lobby to get a drink from the water fountain.

Occasionally a player was still quenching his thirst when play resumed and he had to rush back to the gym. The Big Blues discovered that, in all the excitement of the game, a thirsty player could be conveniently overlooked by the opposing team while he got in position to score an easy lay-up.

"When we came downcourt," recalled Cook, "one of their guys hung back and went out into the lobby for a drink. There were a bunch of people standing outside the door watching and he crouched down behind them.

"They fouled one of our players. As soon as we shot the free throw, one of the Bluefield players grabbed the ball out of bounds and threw it the length of the court. The player who'd been hiding out in the lobby jumped back in, took the long pass, and scored easily since there was no one to guard him."

McDowell scored four of his eight points while playing the lobby position in the final minute of overtime to boost the Big Blues to victory.

"They won it because of that lobby play," complained Cook. "I don't know how many times they got away with it. I didn't realize what had happened the first time. I hadn't seen McDowell run back down the court and I got upset at my players for letting him sneak by them.

"The second time, I had one of my guys on the bench keep his eyes on the Bluefield basket. He saw McDowell run in from the lobby just in time to take the pass and score."

Cook lodged a loud protest with the referees over the lobby play. He argued that Bluefield deserved a technical because a player left the floor. But the refs insisted they hadn't witnessed the violation and allowed McDowell's baskets to count.

Throughout the argument, Bluefield coach Larkin Rucker pleaded innocent.

"Why," grinned Rucker, "there was no trick involved. The boy just asked if he could go get a drink of water a couple of times when things got tense toward the end of the game and I said sure. We're just thankful he made it back in time to catch the long throw and score."

MARIO CUOMO

Forward ○ New York area semi-pro teams ○ 1950s

In politics, New York governor Mario Cuomo has a reputation for being a straight shooter. But during the 1950s, he was anything but that on the basketball court.

That's because when he played amateur and semipro hoops in the New York area, he joined several different teams under several different names. "I played basketball under all sorts of assumed names and in all sorts of leagues," admitted Cuomo in a story he wrote for *Inside Sports.*

He used aliases such as Lava Labretti, Gaylor Esterbrook, Matt Denti, and Glendi LaDuke as a tricky way of getting in extra playing time—and picking up a few extra bucks on the side.

As a student at St. John's prep school, Cuomo was a hoop Palladin: Have basketball, will travel.

On a New Jersey team, Cuomo became Lava Labretti. A friend once asked him why he picked Lava, and Cuomo replied, "Because I'm always hot." When he played with the Austin Celtics in South Jamaica, New York, he was Matt Denti. The name came from his favorite way to prepare pasta, *al dente,* and because, he joked, he was only a half-baked player.

And in Queens, Cuomo's preferred moniker was Glendi LaDuke. The first time he used it, he said, "I had a very hot night. Thirty-six points as Glendi LaDuke.

"I always scored a lot on fouls," Cuomo recalled. "I was not a great player, but I was a very enthusiastic player."

When he suited up for the Austin Celtics, the future politico faced some first-rate competition. In order to even things out, Cuomo and the Celtics weren't above pulling some sneaky shenanigans—such as using "homer" referees and timekeepers to make sure the Celtics had a solid home court advantage.

With their man controlling the clock, a game sped to a quick end, or dragged on forever—depending on whether the Celtics were winning or losing.

Once, Cuomo recalled in the autobiography *Mario Cuomo,* the opposition brought in a ringer, a 6-foot, 4-inch former collegiate star. Cuomo had to guard the high-scoring visitor—an impossible chore without the Celtics' ref to help even things out.

In describing his defense on the big college star, Cuomo recalled, "I hit him, I kneed him, I clawed him, I tackled him. I did everything short of indictable assault, and I wasn't very far from that."

But the partisan official never whistled Cuomo for the flagrant violations. Instead, whenever Cuomo blatantly shoved, tripped, or kicked his opponent, the other guy was always called for the foul. Before the first half ended, the big college star was saddled with four fouls. And with each whistle, a grinning Cuomo went to the free throw line.

"Finally," laughed Cuomo, "we were standing next to each other when somebody else was shooting a foul and this guy turned to the official and yelled, 'Hey, ref. Aren't you going to call a foul on me?' When the ref asked him why, the guy answered, 'Because I'm sweating all over this SOB Cuomo!'"

RICHARD ROBINSON

Reserve ○ University of Nevada–Las Vegas Runnin' Rebels
Jan. 24, 1988

UNLV's Richard Robinson came off the bench to help save the game in the final minute. There was only one problem. He was never actually in the game.

The sly Robinson had leaped off the bench and batted a loose ball back into play to a teammate. The sneaky trick sparked a pivotal three-point play as the Runnin' Rebels knocked the previously undefeated Temple Owls off their perch, 59–58.

Incredibly, Robinson pulled off the chicanery when both officials weren't looking.

With less than a minute to play, the 16–1 Runnin' Rebels trailed the visiting 14–0 Owls by four points, 58–54. Since Temple had the ball, UNLV was in desperate need of a turnover. Suddenly a Rebel defender knocked the ball away from Temple's Mark Macon as he dribbled down the sideline in front of the UNLV bench. But the ball was heading out of bounds and out of the reach of any player on the court.

That's when Robinson entered the game—without checking in. With catlike quickness, he jumped off the bench, tapped the ball back into play, and then sat back down on the bench before the refs and most everyone else knew what he had done.

The Rebs' Keith James then grabbed the loose ball and converted the turnover into a three-point basket that pulled UNLV to 58–57 with 49 seconds left on the clock.

With all the furious action, no one paid any attention to Macon's anguished protests that the ball would have gone out of bounds when it was swatted from his hands, but that someone on the bench had knocked it back in play. Since a Rebel had been the last to touch it, he argued, the ball should have stayed in the Owls' possession.

"The (UNLV) bench tipped that ball back in and the refs didn't see it," Macon complained bitterly after the game.

Following Robinson's bench trick, Temple failed to get a shot to fall the rest of the game. The Runnin' Rebels notched the one-point victory when Anthony Todd hit a turnaround 12-foot jumper with two seconds left.

Robinson helped take credit for the tainted victory. In fact, he bragged about his sneaky trick. "Yes, I did it," he crowed during an interview later on a Las Vegas television station.

Robinson said that both he and teammate Jarvis Basnight, who had fouled out earlier, went for the out-of-bounds ball. "But I beat him to it and knocked it back in to Keith," Robinson said proudly.

Owls coach John Chaney didn't spot the trickery until he reviewed the game film. "We should have been 15–0 after that game," the coach said. "There's no question that Robinson touched the ball. But there was nothing we could do about it."

The loss marred a near-perfect season for the Owls. The only other game they lost all year was to Duke in the NCAA Eastern Regional finals.

ERNIE GRUNFELD

Forward ○ Tennessee Volunteers ○ Jan. 10, 1976

The SEC stands for the Southeastern Conference. But for at least one game, Ernie Grunfeld made it stand for the Southeastern Conspiracy.

Not once but twice the Tennessee sharpshooter sneaked to the free throw line in place of teammates who had been fouled. The volunteering Vol pumped in four points and the sly switcheroo helped whip the Kentucky Wildcats 90–88.

The SEC rivals met in Kentucky's Memorial Coliseum where the ninth-ranked Volunteers hadn't won in nine years. Grunfeld, a 6-foot, 6-inch forward and the team's hottest shooter, was determined to do whatever was necessary to break the losing streak.

Midway through the first half, Kentucky's James Lee was called for fouling Irv Chatman. But when the two teams took their positions for the one-and-one, Grunfeld brazenly stepped to the foul line instead of Chatman and canned both free throws.

Wildcats coach Joe Hall and his bench missed the switch. However, two security officers stationed along the sideline spotted the chicanery and yelled at the officials that the wrong man was shooting the fouls. But their warnings were ignored.

Seven minutes later, Grunfeld decided to repeat his audacious daylight robbery after teammate Bernard King was fouled by Mike Phillips under the Kentucky basket. As the players walked to the other end of the court, King and Grunfeld whispered to each other. When they broke apart, Grunfeld stepped up, took the ball from the unsuspecting ref, and added two more points as Tennessee ended the first half with a 43–42 lead.

During the break, fans who were paying more attention to the game than was the Kentucky bench, got a message through to Hall that he was being shamelessly hoodwinked.

Before the start of the second half, Hall took the complaint to game officials Don Wedge and Red Struthers. The refs confronted Grunfeld with the charge and, to no one's surprise, he denied any hint of cheating.

But with all eyes now on him, Grunfeld didn't dare sneak to the line again. The game went into overtime and thanks to Grunfeld's 43 points—including the four freebies he shot for Chatman and King—the Vols hung on to win 90–88.

The reason for the tricky switch became clear with a check of the game stats. Chatman was 1-for-4 at the line during the game. King went 0-for-1. But Grunfeld had the hot hand. He chucked in 11-for-11 from the charity stripe and 16-of-20 from the floor.

It was too late for Kentucky to file any protest, but Coach Hall got a measure of revenge by exposing the scam on his television program the day after the loss.

"This was a premeditated conspiracy," harrumphed Hall. "The evidence is clear and obvious. I thought it should be exposed." Hall then showed film clips of Grunfeld first talking to Chatman and then to King before taking the foul shots that were not due him.

Rather than deny the charge, Tennessee coach Ray Mears pompously declared, "It's not unusual for a taller man to try to step in on a jump ball or a better foul shooter to go to the line in place of a fellow player."

Retorted Hall, "Is it usual to cheat?"

CHICAGO BULLS

Nov. 13, 1966

The Chicago Bulls followed a devilish strategy to force Wilt Chamberlain out of the game.

During the last quarter of a tight 1966 game, the Bulls ran after Wilt the Stilt and deliberately fouled him even when he didn't have the ball. They chased the Philadelphia 76ers center from back court to front court; from low post to high post. And they hammered him every time they caught up with him.

The fouls were part of a bizarre plot devised by Chicago coach

Johnny Kerr to keep Chamberlain—the league's worst free throw shooter—at the foul line where he could do the least damage. Even though Chamberlain was the most dominant force in the NBA at the time, his free throw tosses were a disgrace to foul shooters everywhere.

Before the game, Kerr and Assistant Coach Al Bianchi were racking their brains trying to figure out how the 7–9 Bulls—the league's newest expansion team—could possibly be competitive with the 10–1 Sixers. The Chicago coaches checked the Philadelphia stat sheet and discovered that while Chamberlain was hitting an astounding 68 percent from the field, he was shooting an abominable 36 percent from the foul line.

The trick to winning, the coaches figured, was to keep Chamberlain at the free throw line so he and his teammates wouldn't get a chance to shoot from the floor.

"Although we'd be in the penalty, we'd still be better off fouling Wilt even if he didn't have the ball," recalled Kerr. "The odds were that he wouldn't make both free throws. But the odds were against us if he shot from the floor."

In the locker room before the game, Kerr told the Bulls, "If we get in a close game and Al and I decide to do something crazy, don't think about it. Just do it."

Midway through the final quarter, the Bulls were down by only six points. Kerr called a time-out and told his players, "Foul Wilt every time he comes over halfcourt on offense. We want him at the foul line."

When play resumed, a herd of foul-minded Bulls chased after Chamberlain wherever he went. On three straight Sixer possessions, Wilt drew the foul, even when he wasn't in the same neighborhood as the ball.

By the third time that he went to the line, Chamberlain had figured out the Chicago plot . . . and he couldn't do anything about it. The more he was fouled, the more upset he became; the more angry he got, the more free throws he missed.

"Wilt started running around in the back court to keep away from our guys, who were chasing him around trying to foul him," recalled Kerr. "He was maybe 50 feet from the ball and half our team was grabbing at him."

Chamberlain ducked and dodged and screamed at the pursuing Bulls, "I'll break your nose if you foul me again!" But the Bulls, egged on by a cheering hometown crowd, were obsessed with fouling the 76ers' all-star. Chamberlain was hacked, pushed, and shoved for six deliberate fouls, but connected on only three of 11 free throws in the quarter.

Amazingly, the sneaky strategy was paying off. Chicago rallied to take a 114–112 lead with 4:23 left in the game. Finally, Philadelphia coach Alex Hannum was forced to bench Chamberlain. The Bulls had virtually fouled Wilt out of the game! Unfortunately for Chicago, Hannum put his best shooters on the floor and the Sixers stormed back to win 132–126.

Hannum grudgingly paid tribute to the Bulls' devious doings. "They were gambling," said Hannum. "Johnny Kerr took a calculated risk and almost pulled one out. It might have worked until I outfoxed him and pulled Wilt out."

Despite the loss, Kerr was delighted with his foul frolic. "Everything had gone almost to perfection," he recalled. "We felt like a couple of tax lawyers who had just found a new loophole that saved our client a million dollars."

Actually, the Chicago coaches were lucky they weren't fined some big bucks. The following day, league officials lowered the boom on them for making a travesty of the game. Kerr was ordered never to pull the stunt again.

And to make sure that the Let's-All-Grab-Wilt gimmick didn't become standard practice, the NBA passed a new rule. Thereafter, any foul away from the ball was a technical. That way, if any team tried to duplicate Chicago's game plan, Philadelphia would use its best shooter for the technical plus get the ball out of bounds.

No team, including the Bulls, ever tried to foul Chamberlain out of a game again.

HEADLESS COACHES

Those who can, do. Those who can't, teach. Those who can't do either, coach. And sometimes they don't do that very well. The lucky ones can mishandle players, draw up a bad play, use the wrong lineup, and still win because they have a talented team. But even if they try to hide behind their won-lost record, their goofs and gaffes become glaring for all to see. For "The Most Foolish Actions of Coaches," The Basketball Hall of SHAME inducts the following:

ELLIS JOHNSON

Coach • Marshall University Thundering Herd • Feb. 5, 1966

No basketball coach ever "put on the dog" quite the way Ellis Johnson did. That's because he literally put on the dog right in the middle of a game.

Doggone if his little stunt didn't end up costing his Marshall University Thundering Herd an important game.

During a 1966 Mid-American Conference clash with the Toledo Rockets in Marshall's Veterans Memorial Field House, Johnson grew increasingly agitated over the officiating of referee Wilson Murray.

Midway in the second half, with Toledo leading 44–35, Wilson called another foul on the Herd, launching Johnson into a tirade. He complained loudly that the officials couldn't do any worse if they had been blindfolded.

Just then, a stray mongrel dog wandered into the midst of the turmoil through an arena door that had been left open. With all the attention focused on the court, no one noticed the floppy-eared, tail-wagging mutt strolling along the baseline.

No one, that is, except Johnson. The coach spotted the black-and-white pooch as it approached the Marshall bench and immediately recognized a once-in-a-lifetime opportunity.

The coach grabbed the stray, plopped it down on his lap, slapped his horn-rimmed glasses on the mutt's nose, and pointed his new "assistant" at Murray. As if on cue, the dog barked right in the referee's face.

Murray got the message loud and clear. And Johnson got a technical foul loud and clear.

Toledo's Jim Cox sank the freebie and the Rockets got possession of the ball—just enough of an edge to help them fend off Marshall in a 70–69 overtime win.

The next day, newspapers ran photos of Johnson and his new animal act. The school's president wasn't amused and ordered the coach to apologize to the community, the opposing team, and the refs, which he did.

"I don't think the technical lost the game for us," said Johnson. "In fact, it fired up our team. Otherwise, we may never have come as close as we did. The official was right in calling a technical on me. But it [the dog stunt] was too good an opportunity to pass up. Maybe I shouldn't have done it. It was one of those things you do on the spur of the moment."

That wasn't the first time Johnson was "T'd" off by an irate official. When he was coaching at Morehead State, Johnson felt his team was getting the short end of the calls in a game against Western Kentucky. Johnson struggled to keep his composure—and his seat—on the bench, but verbally worked over the refs whenever they came within earshot.

Finally, his unsolicited criticism led to the inevitable technical. And that brought Johnson bounding off the bench to go eyeball to eyeball with the official at midcourt.

"After I had my say," recalled Johnson, "the official calmly told me, 'Coach, you've got five seconds to get back to your bench or you'll get a technical foul every time your feet touch the floor on your way.' "

Johnson looked with dismay at the wide expanse of floor separating him from the bench. It was at least 20 feet. So he summoned his two biggest players to join him on the court and ordered them to pick him up by the elbows. The crowd roared with delight as Johnson—with his feet dangling inches above the floor—was carried back to the bench. All it cost him was one more technical foul.

JOHNNY DEE

Coach ○ University of Alabama Crimson Tide ○ Feb. 5, 1955

Johnny Dee was so ticked off at his team's poor play that at halftime he did something no major college coach had ever done before.

He told his players to go fend for themselves—and then walked out on them!

When Dee's Alabama Crimson Tide went to Atlanta to play Georgia Tech in 1955, they were ranked among the top ten teams in the nation and were on a 15-game winning streak. But in the first half, they were getting stung badly by the lowly Yellow Jackets.

"We were pretty cocky because we had been beating everybody like a drum," recalled 'Bama guard Leon Marlaire. "But before we knew it, Georgia Tech had us down by 13 points at halftime. We looked terrible. And if there was one thing that Johnny Dee really hated it was that kind of lackadaisical play. We knew he'd be laying for us at halftime, but we got the surprise of our lives."

At the break, Dee stormed into the locker room. Then, to everyone's bewilderment, he marched right past his team and into the showers. There, all alone, he raged at each player in turn as if they were standing in front of him.

"Marlaire, you couldn't guard your lunch!" shouted Dee.

Chastising All-America center Jerry Harper, who was sitting in the next room, Dee snarled, "Harper, why don't you go to the bathroom in the middle of the court so you can at least say you did *something* out there!"

After ripping his starters, Dee stomped back into the locker room. "We thought he had it all out of his system, but then he really went crazy," recalled Marlaire. "He started to diagram a play on the blackboard, but something set him off again and he rammed his fist clean through that old board."

With the blackboard in shambles and his team quaking in their sneakers, Dee still wasn't finished. He told his players he was too ashamed to be seen in public with them and that they'd just have to go back out onto the court and coach themselves. With that said, Dee disappeared into the showers again.

"We thought he was kidding," said Marlaire. "But when the five-minute warning call came, Dee yelled that he wasn't going to be a part of the disgrace and wasn't coming out."

The stunned Alabama players returned to the court and warmed up, thinking that Dee would reappear at any minute. But at tip-off time, the coach was still nowhere to be seen. So the players decided among themselves to keep the same starting five on the floor.

"We were scared to death, because in the past Dee had pretty much told us every move to make on the court," said Marlaire. "We decided we'd better start playing some ball or Dee would really be hell to live with when we got back home."

With five minutes left in the game, Alabama's coachless five—still calling their own plays and setting the game strategy—had cut the Georgia Tech lead to a few points. The crowd noise intensified, and the suspense finally drew Dee out of the shower room. The missing coach then sneaked around the corner of the door leading to the gym.

"We saw Dee peeking at us back there," said Marlaire. "Then, when we finally pulled ahead, out he comes on the dead run, yelling for a time-out. He got in the middle of the huddle, slapped each of us in the face, and yelled, 'By God, now this is my team!'

"Personally, I was embarrassed. I'd never heard of a coach hiding in the locker room before."

Incredibly, whatever Dee's motives were, his absence worked. Alabama rallied to a 76–72 victory.

Recalled Dee, "The thing that bothered me most of all was that

Georgia Tech sent me a bill for $22 to pay for the blackboard I punched."

IN YOUR FACE!

University of Michigan coach Bill Frieder nearly booted his top assistant, Steve Fisher, off the team in 1987.

A few days before the Wolverines were to play Iowa, Frieder noticed his team was practicing poorly. "There was not enough concentration and I really got mad, yelling and swearing and ranting and raving," he recalled.

The players and Fisher were facing Frieder in a semicircle. As Frieder worked himself into a lather, he saw a basketball on the floor and kicked it as hard as he could.

"Fisher couldn't have been more than five feet away from me and it caught him point-blank in the face," Frieder recalled. "He went down for the count and we all thought he was dead. Fortunately, all he had was a black eye and a bunch of bruises. But I guess I got their attention."

FRANK LAYDEN

Coach ○ Utah Jazz ○ March 12, 1985

With his team getting blown out by the Los Angeles Lakers, Utah Jazz coach Frank Layden figured there wasn't much he could do . . . so, during the game, he walked out of the arena and went across the street for a sandwich!

Midway in the fourth quarter of a 123–108 defeat at the hands of the Lakers at the Forum, Layden's mind started to wander. He began thinking about the great chili and the bacon, lettuce, and tomato sandwiches served at the coffee shop of the team's hotel.

"We were getting killed by the Lakers—as usual," recalled the NBA's funniest coach. "The Los Angeles fans were—and still are—notorious for coming late and leaving early. So, during this one game, while there were still several minutes left to play, I looked around and saw all these people walking out. So I asked myself, 'What the heck am I staying for?' "

With the game totally out of reach, Layden turned to his assistant,

Andrew D. Bernstein/NBA Photos

Phil Johnson, and told him, "I'll see you later. Try to pull this one out." Johnson's jaw dropped as Layden got off the bench and started to walk away.

As the hungry coach passed the Los Angeles bench, Lakers coach Pat Riley, looking perplexed, asked Layden, "Where are you going, Frank? Did you get thrown out of the game when I wasn't looking?"

Layden shook his head. "No," he replied. "I'm just going across the street to grab a drink, some chili, and a BLT. You want to come along?"

"You've got to be kidding," said Riley.

"No, really, I'm leaving," said Layden. Pointing to the stands, he told Riley, "Everybody else is leaving and since we're getting beat so badly, I don't see why I should have to sit here all alone and suffer through it."

Layden then sauntered out of the Forum and headed across the street to the coffee shop, where he ordered a bowl of chili and a BLT on rye. Recalled Layden, "The guy at the counter told me, 'You know, this is amazing. You look exactly like Frank Layden, the coach from Utah. He's staying here in the hotel. Stick around. He'll probably be in here later after the game is over.' I just nodded."

Word eventually got around Los Angeles that Layden had skipped out early with the fans. Recalled the coach (shown joking with the

Lakers' Mychal Thompson), "The next time the Jazz played at the Forum, the fans yelled at me, 'Hey, Frank, is it time to leave yet?'"

ADOLPH RUPP

Coach ○ University of Kentucky Wildcats ○ 1931–72

Adolph Rupp—the winningest coach in college basketball history—slam-dunked his players with words that left them hurting but laughing.

It was easier for his Kentucky Wildcats to handle a full-court press than it was to cope with his caustic criticisms, razor-sharp barbs, and sarcastic put-downs.

Nothing short of perfection mattered to Rupp, who compiled an astonishing 875–190 record. Recalled Boston Celtics coach Red Auerbach, "I remember one night when Kentucky won a game in Madison Square Garden. But they looked so bad winning it that Rupp waited for everyone to leave the building. Then he had the lights turned on again and started a practice at midnight."

To Rupp, practice was a time for players like Jack Tucker to pay for the sins they committed during the previous game. Tucker's transgres-

sion was missing four free throws in a 1934 game against the University of Cincinnati. The following Monday during practice, Rupp yelled, "Tucker, come here! Get that chair and place it on the foul line. Now you sit there the rest of the afternoon and look at that basket." The humiliated Tucker spent all of practice sitting in the chair while his teammates snickered.

One salvo from Rupp's tongue could humble the cockiest player. During an early-season practice scrimmage in 1954, Rupp was riding 6-foot guard Gayle Rose about his failure to get a rebound. Finally, after two hours, Rose grabbed a rebound and proudly dribbled the ball up the court. "Rose!" yelled Rupp. "You look like a Shetland pony in a stud horse parade. Stop practice, everyone, and take a shower. We're going to have a successful season now. Rose got a rebound!"

At times Rupp's desire for perfect practices bordered on heartlessness. In the fall of 1941, Kentucky guard Vince Splane received permission to leave the team to attend the funeral of his grandmother. A few days after Splane's return, Coach Rupp lambasted the team over a lousy practice. "My God, boys, we're not going to continue playing like this. This is war!" Then he singled out Splane. "And another thing. We're not going to have any more of this grandmother dying business."

Rupp was at his scorching, scathing best—or worst—during halftime, as Ed Beck learned firsthand.

Beck was recruited from the state of Georgia, one of the few Wildcats to come from outside Kentucky. During a game against the University of Mississippi in 1957, the Wildcats were trailing by six points at halftime. Rupp chastised each player. When he got to Beck, the ranting coach said, "Ed, I want you to go to the hotel right now and write me a letter, no, write me a theme, no, better make that a doctorate dissertation on this subject: 'Why Adolph Rupp was crazy enough to go to the state of Georgia after the likes of you.'" Fortunately, Beck didn't have to write the paper. He and his teammates were so hurt by Rupp's put-downs that they took out their anger on Mississippi and won.

During the 1944–45 season, Coach Rupp came into the locker room at halftime with his squad leading Arkansas State 34–4. He bolted through the door and stared glumly at the scorebook while his players wondered how he could possibly be critical of their performance. He noticed that one Arkansas State player had scored all the team's four points. "Who's guarding number twelve?" Rupp asked angrily.

Jack Parkinson looked up and said, "I am, Coach."

"Well, get on him, because he's running absolutely wild!" Rupp thundered. Kentucky won 75–6.

Victory did not protect the Wildcats from Rupp's sharp-tongued cuts, as Terry Mobley painfully discovered. In 1962, Kentucky played poorly and barely managed to beat Temple at the Palestra in Philadelphia. Mobley and Rupp were walking off the floor together when the coach said, "Mobley, would you please go back to the middle of the floor and just sit there until I can get the hell out of this place?"

"Coach, I always try to do what you say, but I don't quite understand," replied Mobley.

Rupp glowered at him and said, "I want you to be able to tell the folks back in Lexington that you did something good and constructive here in Philadelphia."

During games, sympathetic words were not a part of Rupp's vocabulary, according to Pat Riley, former coach of the Los Angeles Lakers, who played for Rupp from 1965–67. "During one game, I drove hard to the basket, missed the shot, got the rebound, missed again and again and again," Riley recalled. "I got creamed on the final rebound but no foul was called and I was knocked to the floor and slid right in front of Coach Rupp. I was lying on the floor exhausted, hoping for a little compassion from him. He looked down at me, looked out on the floor, and then said, 'Pat, get your ass up! There goes your man with the ball!'"

For a coach who preached that hard work leads to victory, Rupp was extremely superstitious. He always wore a lucky brown suit to the games. And he had this thing about hairpins—he was convinced they brought good luck. Hours before a game, he would look for hairpins that had fallen on the sidewalk or in the playing arena. To him, the more hairpins he found, the better his team was going to play.

In 1956, the Wildcats trounced Temple University in Philadelphia's Palestra, which had been the venue for a stage show the previous night. Before the game, Rupp learned that the dressing room had been used by women, so he scoured the floor for hairpins. Suddenly he shouted with glee because he had found a box of hairpins. "We're going to have a helluva game tonight!" he loudly announced.

"Coach, you're not superstitious, are you?" asked one of his players.

"No," Rupp replied. "I learned a long time ago that it's bad luck to be superstitious."

JOE LAPCHICK

Coach ○ St. John's University Redmen–New York Knicks ○ 1936–65

Joe Lapchick had a unique method of dealing with the stress of coaching—he fainted. Usually at courtside, sometimes in the locker room, and occasionally in his office.

He suffered from a nervous stomach and jangled nerves and coached as if every game was a matter of life and death. "The trouble with you," a doctor once told Lapchick, "is that day after day, you're suffering what the average person suffers once or twice in a lifetime."

Lapchick's most famous faint came midway through the championship game of the 1944 National Invitational Tournament, when his St. John's University Redmen were defending their title against DePaul University.

The Blue Demons were ahead by three points when Lapchick leaped to his feet to protest a call—and fainted dead away. For several minutes, Lapchick lay prone between the two benches while DePaul coach Ray Meyer hovered over him like a worried mother hen.

UPI/Bettmann

After a brief interruption the game continued while Lapchick lay blissfully oblivious to the action on the court. Every time Redmen's captain Hy Gotkin dribbled past the St. John's bench, he anxiously called out, "Are you OK, Coach? Are you OK?"

Bill Esposito, St. John's sports information director under Lapchick, recalled that with the coach flat on his back, the Redmen surged into the lead. When he finally came around, Lapchick glanced at the scoreboard and discovered his team had built a ten-point advantage and was wrapping up its second straight championship.

Later, Lapchick muttered, "When I fainted, we were behind. When I woke up, we were ahead. That dealt coaching one hell of a blow."

Lapchick also passed out when he was coaching the New York Knicks. In 1952 the Knicks were romping to what appeared to be an easy win over the underdog Fort Wayne Pistons. But then Lapchick watched in horror as the Pistons chipped away at the New York lead and won the game in the final seconds.

The coach staggered off the court like a man in a trance. Lapchick made it to the locker room before passing out, and then spent the next three days in the hospital recovering from the shock of the loss.

He wound up in the hospital again from another fainting spell caused when he had to cut a player. It was a distasteful chore that always left Lapchick emotionally drained. A few minutes after notifying former Seton Hall player Tommy Byrne that he hadn't made the Knicks' squad, the coach hit the floor in a dead faint—and spent another week in the hospital settling his nerves.

"Joe fainted a lot because he was a very excitable guy," said Esposito. "We played most of our games in Madison Square Garden, where smoking was allowed. Joe was so nervous he'd smoke an entire pack of Pall Mall cigarettes during the game. Sometimes all you could see was this cloud of smoke down there on the end of the bench where the coach was sitting."

Because most every game brought him untold agony, Lapchick had little control over his emotions.

One time, the Knicks blew a 12-point lead with only five minutes left in the game and lost. Lapchick broke into sobs and didn't stop crying until he went home. The next day, he remembered nothing of what had happened except that the Knicks had blown the game.

Frequently, when a call went against his team, the coach jumped to his feet, tore off his suit coat, and hurled it toward the bench. Usually he missed. His jacket ended up wrapped around some spectator's head and one of Lapchick's embarrassed assistants had to ask for it back.

"Many times Joe picked up a water cup and, after taking a sip, just threw the nearly full cup in the general direction of the water bucket at the end of the bench," recalled Esposito. "Whoever was nearby usually got drenched, so players fought over who had to sit closest to the water."

Once, during a Knicks game, Lapchick was getting a drink from a tray of water cups when a play on the floor upset him. The coach seized the entire tray, tossed it straight up in the air—and got the surprise of his life when the tray, cups, and water came straight down on his noggin.

Lapchick was as famous for his superstitions as for his nervousness. During the 1961–62 season, after Lapchick had returned from the pros to coach the Redmen again, St. John's won the last 11 games of the regular season.

Lapchick didn't change his shirt during the entire streak. He would show up at the arena in a clean shirt but change to his smelly lucky shirt before the game started.

"Joe wore that same shirt every game for the rest of the year," said Esposito. "When the season finally ended, Mrs. Lapchick said she carried that shirt out to the garbage with ice tongs."

DOUG MOE

Coach ○ Denver Nuggets ○ Nov. 22, 1983

Denver coach Doug Moe concocted the most shameful defense ever seen in the NBA—the stand-aside-and-watch defense.

In the final minute of a 1983 game, the coach audaciously ordered his Nuggets to surrender unconditionally and let the Portland Trail Blazers score at will.

Denver was getting creamed 146–116 when Moe called a time-out with 1:12 left in the game. The hometown Portland fans, hoping to see their Blazers break the team scoring record of 150 points, screamed for blood.

In the Nuggets' huddle, Moe acted like Mr. Nice Guy to his enemy and Mr. Meanie to his team. Willing to help Portland and hoping to shame his players for their poor defense, he told them, "Back off and let them have it [the scoring record]." He ordered the Nuggets to

launch shots as quickly as possible and offer no defensive resistance whatsoever.

When play resumed, the Nuggets did what they were told. Portland ran off five uncontested lay-ups while the Denver players stood back and watched. The Blazers got their record and a 156–116 victory. "Our defense was getting so tenacious, I was afraid they weren't going to get 150," joked Moe following the game. "I really was scared." Acknowledging the surrender tactics, Moe said, "There wasn't much difference between that defense and the way we were before."

Besides, he added, the fans loved it. "They enjoy a little massacre. People like blood. We play 82 games and if you're not ready—especially against a team as good as Portland—what are you going to do? Get out the whips and chains?"

The Nuggets, who suffered one of their worst off nights ever, took Moe's absurd instructions with good humor. Said Denver forward Kenny Dennard, "It was hilarious what Doug did. We were playing like crap. As if a minute and 12 seconds makes a difference in a game like that." Echoed guard Rob Williams, "It was funny."

The league office didn't think so. It fined Moe $5,000, suspended him for two games, and gave him a severe tongue lashing. Scotty Stirling, the league's vice president of operations, blistered Moe in a letter informing him of the stiff fine and suspension. "To simply allow a team five uncontested baskets is to make a travesty of the game and to seriously tarnish the image of the NBA, your team, and your profession," wrote Stirling.

Moe claimed that the Nuggets' defense was so horrendous throughout the game that the outcome would have been the same even without waving the white flag. He insisted that his order to lie down in the final 72 seconds was meant to embarrass the Nuggets for playing so rotten all night.

"I have no qualms about what I did," said Moe after learning of the suspension. "If anything, it's helped the team. We're playing better defensively now and I don't feel badly about it."

Maybe giving up didn't bother the losing coach, but it sure did bother the winning coach. Enraged by Moe's no-defense defense, Portland coach Jack Ramsay sent a letter to all the other NBA coaches reminding them of their responsibilities in upholding the integrity of the game.

Said Denver assistant coach Bill Ficke, who took over for Moe during the suspension, "What Doug did wasn't really wrong. He just needed to find a better way to do it."

BOBBY KNIGHT

Coach ○ Indiana Hoosiers ○ March 8, 1981

As if the state rivalry between Purdue and Indiana wasn't heated enough, Hoosier coach Bobby Knight added fuel to the fire during one of his weekly television shows.

Knight had publicly stated that the basketball crowds at Purdue were more abusive, more obnoxious, and more obscene than anywhere else in the Big Ten. When the Hoosiers played at Mackey Arena in West Lafayette, Indiana, in 1981, Knight had been the butt of vulgar remarks from the crowd.

After the game, Purdue athletic director George King apologized for the boorish actions of the Boilermaker fans. But Knight wasn't appeased. He held a press conference in which he denounced "the Purdue mentality."

Then the day after the Hoosiers clinched the 1981 Big Ten championship, Knight stuck it to Purdue during his television show. He told the audience that he had a special guest who was substituting for King, who had declined to appear on the show. Knight said the substitute guest "probably would express the same ideas" as King and would be "symbolic of the Purdue fans."

Then the camera switched to his guest—a live mule! And it was wearing a Purdue cap. "His first name is Jack," said Knight. "I'll let you figure out the last name."

Knight fought hard to control his laughter when the guest, apparently nervous about appearing on statewide TV, left a memento on the studio floor.

Knight's show riled Boilermaker supporters in West Lafayette, as he had intended. He defended his barnyard humor by pointing out that his guest wasn't as crude as the Purdue fans who had yelled obscenities at him and his players.

Later, when the Hoosiers returned from Philadelphia after winning the NCAA title, Knight got another kick out of his mule stunt. During a campus celebration at Assembly Hall in Bloomington, Knight told the crowd, "We were going to bring Jack with us. But he was up north visiting his brothers, Half and Wise."

Up north, in this case, meant West Lafayette.

BOOING THE BOOSTERS

Fans come to the arena to watch a game and engage in one of America's favorite pastimes—booing. At the whistle-happy ref, the fumble-fingered dribbler, the air-ball free throw shooter. Sometimes, however, the real boos shouldn't be directed toward the basketball court, but right up to the stands where fans have displayed some of the rowdiest conduct this side of a riot zone. For "The Most Outlandish Behavior of Fans," The Basketball Hall of SHAME inducts the following:

CENTRAL MICHIGAN CHIPPEWAS FANS
1986–88

Central Michigan fans didn't squeeze the Charmin—they threw it. Tons of it.

In one of the most bizarre fan rituals ever, the crowd at each home game flung thousands of rolls of toilet paper onto the court the instant the Chippewas scored their first basket.

It looked as if a mammoth indoor blizzard had swept through Central Michigan's Dan Rose Arena. Massive streamers of tissue littered the floor, dangled from the rafters, festooned the baskets, and halted games for about five minutes while cleanup crews hauled away huge bags of unraveled toilet paper.

The zany practice started in the mid-1980s when a few disgruntled fans tossed a couple of rolls as an expression of disgust over the team's lousy play. But when Central Michigan started winning, TP tossing took on a whole new meaning. It became the fans' way of saying that the Chippewas were going to wipe up every opponent in sight.

By 1987, the toilet paper cannonade had mushroomed from a handful of rolls to hundreds, then thousands, of Mr. Whipple's finest.

Robert Barclay/Central Michigan University Media Relations

Peggy Brisbane/Central Michigan University Media Relations

The bombardment covered the entire arena in a sea of white—with streaks of blue and pink thrown in for variety. Sports information director Fred Stabley, Jr., estimated that 5,000 rolls a game were hurled onto the court during the peak of the craziness.

"At one point a toilet paper company even set up shop at the front door and handed out free samples to anyone who hadn't brought a roll to throw," recalled Stabley.

At the opening tip-off most of the 6,000 spectators—faculty included—stood and waved their ammunition, waiting for the signal to fire. Then, as soon as the Chippewas scored, players on both sides dashed for cover.

"It was incredible," marveled Chippewas star Dan Majerle. "You'd look up from the floor and see nothing but white toilet paper covering everything."

The demand for toilet paper of any color became so great that stores in the Mount Pleasant area ordered extra stock in anticipation of a run on the precious commodity. Overnight, supplies disappeared from public rest rooms throughout Central Michigan. Students hoarded toilet paper, swiping rolls from rest rooms of student dorms, buildings, and even the arena itself.

Sometimes the paper shortage reached the crisis point. The team's equipment manager, Dan Bookey, recalled when a student rushed up to him at halftime of one game, begging for a roll of toilet paper. "He wasn't interested in throwing it," said Bookey. "The poor guy really needed a roll. We had a couple hidden away in the equipment room, so I helped him out."

Recycling became the rage. Fans volunteered to serve on the cleanup crews at the arena as a means of augmenting their supplies of TP during periods of extreme shortage.

Athletic Director Dave Keilitz said, "We realized how far it had gone when we'd see 65-year-old ladies come to the games clutching their ticket in one hand and a roll of toilet paper in the other."

Halfway through the 1987–88 season, officials of the Mid-American Conference decided to ban toilet papering. A special regulation—the Central Michigan Rule—was passed, which mandated a technical foul on the home team at the first sight of thrown toilet paper. The new rule went into effect just before Central Michigan played Cleveland State in 1988. The ban worked. Not a roll was thrown.

"It was fun while it lasted," said Stabley. It was also a portent of good luck. The Chippewas won 14 straight home games in which toilet paper had been tossed. But right after the ban, the team was only 3–3 at home.

INDIANA PACER STRIPPERS

Feb. 18, 1981

Four female fanatics bared their hearts, souls—and breasts—to show their support for the Indiana Pacers.

Led by a topless dancer named Trixie, the buxom beauties instigated a near riot in Indianapolis' Market Square Arena when they stripped to the waist during a 1981 game against the visiting Atlanta Hawks.

Throughout the contest the foursome, equipped with huge cowbells and equally huge boobs, thoroughly upstaged the more sedate Pacer cheerleaders, the Pace-Mates. While the Pace-Mates attempted to perform their routines during time-outs, the quartet put on an unsolicited titillating show of their own in the aisles. Dressed in scanty costumes that were held together with little more than spit and postage stamps, the foursome did their own bump and grind that even caught the attention of the players.

The gals didn't expose their true forms until the Pacers called the game's final time-out. That was the signal for the bosomy beauties to go into their "grind" finale. With cowbells clanging, the four leaped into the air and flamboyantly stripped off their tops.

What decorum was left in the Arena vanished in the uproar over the unveiling.

Cops rushed to the impromptu peel-off and arrested the four offenders. The crowd, now more engrossed in the off-court performance than in the boring game, hooted and booed the policemen as they draped the quartet's chests and hustled them off to jail.

(An Indianapolis police spokesman said the four were later released when the Pacers refused to press charges. "The Pacers figured it might boost attendance if word got out they had free strippers instead of a winning team," joked one cop.)

While the teams and officials waited for the turmoil to subside so they could finish the game, referee Earl Strom stood on the floor and amusedly watched the sideshow unfold.

A woman in a courtside seat, as outraged over the exhibition as Strom was delighted, shook a finger in the veteran official's face. "That's disgusting," she snorted.

"It certainly is," Strom said with a smile.

"Then why are you still watching it?" she asked.

"Madam," Strom patiently explained, "I'm trying to determine just *how* disgusting it is."

LET'S JEER IT FOR THE FANS

• When Georgia Tech's Dennis Scott—a player who had recently shed 30 pounds—was introduced at a 1990 game at Duke, the students there showered the court with Twinkies, bagels, and doughnuts. Duke coach Mike Krzyzewski immediately apologized to the Georgia Tech team.

• When Austin Peay (pronounced like "pea") advanced in the 1987 NCAA basketball tournament, one of the school's chants reportedly led to massive tie-ups at the rest rooms. That's because fans of the small school kept shouting, "Let's go Peay!"

• Hotheaded University of Pittsburgh coach Doc Carlson was furious over the officiating during a 1949 game at West Virginia. Every time the whistle blew against his team, he stood up and shouted, "That burns me up!" Finally when he said it one time too many, he was soaked with a bucket of ice water—compliments of two West Virginia fans.

• New Mexico lost a home game to Texas–El Paso in 1986 because of a paper cup. New Mexico led 70–69 with two seconds left when UTEP's Wayne Campbell stepped to the foul line for a one-and-one opportunity. Campbell released his first shot as a paper cup flew by him. He missed the free throw and the game would have ended, except the referee voided the shot because the player was distracted. Campbell then sank two straight free throws to give UTEP a 71–70 win.

• During a 1952 NBA game in Fort Wayne, referee Chuck Solodare was the target of exceptional verbal abuse from the fans. Shortly before the end of the game, Solodare pulled a raw steak from inside his shirt, tossed it to the crowd, and shouted, "Here, you wolves, chew on that for a while."

JACK NICHOLSON

Actor ○ Los Angeles Lakers Fan

Jack Nicholson rates an Oscar without even acting—as the most outrageous celebrity fan in the NBA.

The Academy Award winner for *One Flew Over the Cuckoo's Nest* has goosed an opposing coach during a game and mooned fans during a championship series.

The ardent Lakers supporter, who has a permanent front-row seat at the Forum, got into his most infamous courtside altercation when he goosed Dallas Mavericks coach Dick Motta late in the first half of a game in 1980.

"I stepped onto the court and yelled instructions to my team, when I felt someone hold my leg and then goose me," Motta recalled. "I looked down and there was this guy on his hands and knees. I didn't know who he was at first. He looked like some seedy old bum. I started kicking the guy and punching him to make him let go. Finally the security people came running over and separated us.

"At halftime, they told me that was Jack Nicholson and that I should be more polite in how I treated him. That made me mad. So I went up to Nicholson and told him, 'Don't ever touch me again or I'll smear your face all over the cuckoo's nest. You won't need a frontal lobotomy when I get through with you.'

"He said, 'I just got excited because you were breaking the rules when you went onto the court.'"

Motta responded by offering to make Nicholson an assistant coach so he would at least work for his seat.

When Los Angeles makes the play-offs, Nicholson usually follows the Lakers on their road games and acts as the team's most vocal cheerleader. But more than once he has acted more like a jeerleader in the Boston Garden during the Lakers-Celtics finals.

During the 1984 NBA Finals, which Boston won four games to three, Garden officials made sure Nicholson was kept far from the action. Instead of the courtside seat he enjoys in Los Angeles, the actor was banished to a box in the balcony high above the Garden floor.

In the final game, when it was obvious the Lakers were about to suffer a 111–102 defeat, Nicholson expressed his affection for the Boston fans by flipping them off, according to several Boston reporters. Then, when the mob howled for his hide, Nicholson whipped out a few more gestures.

AP/Wide World Photos

"Jack flashed some obscene body language at the Garden crowd," recalled Kareem Abdul-Jabbar in his book, *Kareem*. "When it became clear we were going to lose, Jack, from his conspicuous spot above the Garden floor, grabbed his crotch in an inciteful gesture toward the whole sea of Celtics fans. . . . He had the whole fifteen thousand screaming at him."

When the Lakers returned to Boston to resume the intense championship rivalry in 1985, the Celtics fans were waiting for Nicholson. They gave him the choke sign and wore T-shirts that carried Nicholson's picture with the words "Hit the road, Jack." Nicholson just flashed that devilish smile of his.

He got his revenge when the Lakers drubbed the Celtics 111–100 to win the championship four games to two. But the final game was best remembered in Boston not for the Celtics' defeat but as the year of the Nicholson moon.

According to sportswriters Scott Ostler and Steve Spring in their book, *Winnin' Times,* Nicholson ". . . stirred up Celtics fans and was even accused of mooning the Boston Garden crowd. Although taped replays are inconclusive, the mooning has become part of Laker-Celtic legend."

Boston Globe sportswriter and columnist Bob Ryan said the moon has become fixed in Garden lore because so many fans claim to have witnessed it.

"Jack was sitting in the first row of seats in the luxury boxes opposite the Celtics' bench," recalled Ryan. "The Celtics fans were laying for him and they started chanting 'Jack . . . Jack.' That's when he supposedly turned around and showed them his better side."

Boston Globe photographer Janet Knott said she saw the moon but missed getting a picture of it because she was too far away. "Nicholson was giving it back to the fans all through the series," recalled Knott. "He was acting wilder and crazier than any of the Boston people. I didn't have my camera on him when the moon came out. It would have been a great picture, but since we're a family newspaper, I doubt if we would have run a photo of Jack Nicholson's butt."

TRINITY BANTAMS FANS
Feb. 24, 1954

In one of the fowlest games ever played, fans of tiny Trinity College gave mighty Yale the bird—a few dozen times.

Students from the small school in Hartford, Connecticut, were tired of being looked down upon by their haughty neighbors from New Haven. The Elis often delighted in poking fun at the Trinity nickname—the Bantams. So when Yale agreed to play the Bantams in the Elis' Payne Whitney Gymnasium, a bunch of Trinity tricksters decided to tweak the blue Yalie noses.

On game night, about 300 Trinity students arrived on the Yale campus, many wearing large overcoats and carrying gym bags and instrument cases. The students quietly took seats scattered throughout the balcony overlooking the court. And then they waited.

Yale took the opening tip-off and quickly scored. Then Trinity inbounded and carefully worked the ball in to center Matt Wallace in the key. Wallace drove the lane and scored the Bantams' first goal—and that was the signal for the Trinity fans to go into action.

Overcoats were flung aside, instrument cases and gym bags popped open, and out flew several dozen squawking, flapping, feather-shedding chickens. Startled players and officials scurried for cover as the birds rained down on the court from the overhead balcony.

"I thought it was just about the funniest sight I had ever seen," recalled Trinity coach Ray Oosting, still chuckling over the wild commotion that interrupted the game.

"Everywhere you looked there were chickens flying out of the balcony. I later learned that they were supposed to be bantam roosters, since Trinity was known as the Bantams. But those city kids couldn't tell a bantam from a bullfrog, so they threw anything that had feathers and clucked.

"Somehow they had smuggled all those chickens into the gym without arousing any suspicions. When we scored that first goal, the students jumped up and started tossing chickens out of the balcony. The whole place was full of flying feathers."

Oosting may have found the stunt hilarious, but Elis coach Howard Hobson didn't see anything humorous about turning his beloved gym into a henhouse.

Hobson rushed to the Trinity bench. "What the hell do you think you're doing?" Hobson stormed at Oosting. "You put them up to this!"

Oosting protested his innocence and sent his team out to help Yale players, fans, and officials round up the flock of runaway cluckers.

"They had to delay the game several minutes," recalled Oosting. "And by the time they got all the chickens gathered up, the floor was a mess. They had to clean it up before we could get back to basketball.

"Yale won [75–66], as expected. But our students showed them a good time. And it was the last time Yale ever made fun of the Bantams."

ROBIN FICKER

Washington Bullets Fan ○ 1984–present

If there's one fan that NBA players would love to gag, it's Robin Ficker. And he's proud of it.

The Washington Bullets' rabid rooter occupies a permanent seat behind the visitors' bench at the Capital Centre and makes life miserable for opposing coaches and players.

He has bullied, berated, and bad-mouthed them with such intensity that league officials even investigated Ficker . . . and concluded they couldn't do a thing to shut him up.

Not that the players haven't tried.

Michael Jordan threw a ball at him; Isiah Thomas threw a shoe; and James Worthy threw a towel. The Golden State Warriors tossed

Gatorade at him and the Indiana Pacers tossed water. And Utah Jazz coach Frank Layden threw a fit.

In 1989 the Philadelphia 76ers erected a canvas banner behind their bench to try to protect the players from Ficker and his barrage of insults during time-outs. Most teams move their time-out huddles onto the court away from the bench just to get away from Ficker's shrill, nonstop harangues.

"I contribute a lot to the game," said Ficker, an attorney from Bethesda, Maryland. "I keep up a constant chatter and these guys can't get away from it. I use emotional karate on them. When they're down, I take 'em down even further—anybody in foul trouble, anybody getting a hard time from the coach, anybody who's had some bad publicity in the press."

Ficker's attacks on players' personal lives—including their wives and girlfriends—is what makes him so universally disliked among visiting NBA teams.

"I do my homework so I know who's vulnerable, who's having a slump, who's got problems in their personal lives," he said. "And then I go right for the jugular."

Ficker's seat is so close to the players that he's practically in the visitors' huddle—and during time-outs he cranks up the volume to disrupt them.

"I'm right there on top of the teams," Ficker said. "It's not just the loudness that gets to them, it's the constant repetition. I never let up.

"I can see the coach drawing the plays, so I contradict everything he says. I yell at the players why a play won't work or that they don't have to listen to that jerk of a coach. They're trying to take a breather and get some instructions, but I'm right there bad-mouthing everything the coach tells them. I distract them any way I can so they won't have their minds on the game."

So many coaches complained about Ficker's blaring distractions that the NBA videotaped him during a game and sent the league's security chief, Horace Balmer, to sit nearby and spy on Ficker.

Later, Rod Thorn, the NBA's director of operations, said the league couldn't curb Ficker's heckling, no matter how irritating it might be to the players.

"He's loud, I'll say that," said Thorn. "But he doesn't curse and he doesn't leave his seat area. It doesn't seem to bother the people sitting around him. If he were abusive, or if people were upset, maybe we could get him out of there, but there's nothing we can do."

No, but players and coaches still try. The usually unflappable Frank Layden became so incensed over Ficker's continual insults and interruptions that during one game in 1986 he charged after the loudmouth and had to be restrained by assistant coaches. "And Layden was the most easygoing coach ever," said Jazz spokesman Kim Turner.

"Everybody in the league knows about him [Ficker] and most players have been warned to stay away from him no matter how badly he needles them."

Sometimes, though, they can't help themselves.

"The Indiana Pacers throw a lot of water," said Ficker. "And [Pacers forward] LaSalle Thompson spits on me every chance he gets."

Philadelphia's Charles Barkley once stood up on a chair, glowered at Ficker, and heckled back. "Barkley said that George Bush and I were the two biggest jerks in Washington—only jerk wasn't exactly the term he used," recalled Ficker.

When the Warriors doused their tormentor with Gatorade, Ficker responded with even more taunts. "I told them I didn't care what they threw at me as long as they lost, since they were all a bunch of losers anyway," said Ficker. "And then I reminded [Warriors forward] Chris Mullin that I was the only thing he'd hit all night.

"Isiah Thomas threw a shoe at me and James Worthy threw a towel trying to get me to keep quiet. They both missed. Naturally, I just heckled them that much louder.

"Michael Jordan once threw a ball at me because I got on him about his hair loss. He's sensitive about that and keeps his hair cut short to hide it. Sometimes when he makes a basket, he rubs his head and looks over at me. I also call him 'Air Ball Jordan' a lot."

Ficker said Magic Johnson used to ignore him, "but I started calling him 'Coca-Cola' after he bought a Pepsi franchise, so now I'm getting under his skin.

"Larry Bird cusses me a lot. He calls me a faggot. I call him Larry Nerd and get on him about getting old and slow. He's got a short fuse so it's easy to get him mad."

In his book, *Drive,* Bird summed up the players' opinion of the Mouth that Roared by saying, "If there was an open season on fans, he'd be the first one I'd bag."

VANDERBILT FANS

Jan. 25, 1989

With a two-point lead, the Vanderbilt Commodores were just one second away from beating Florida and tightening their hold on first place in the Southeastern Conference.

But Vandy's own fans spoiled the triumph by heaving a last-second barrage of yellow tennis balls onto the court. Their premature prank backfired, with ruinous results. It cost Vanderbilt the game and, ultimately, the conference championship.

"Those weren't Vanderbilt fans," fumed Vandy coach C. M. Newton. "They were a couple of damn yokels who got carried away.

"It was the toughest loss I've ever been associated with. All we had to do with one second left was inbound the ball, but all of a sudden there we were in overtime."

The tennis ball stunt was a way of taunting the Gators' center, Dwayne Schintzius. During the preseason, Schintzius had been accused of threatening another Florida student with a tennis racket during a campus spat. After the season opened, Schintzius-bashing became a popular indoor sport wherever the Gators played. He was the frequent target of tennis balls thrown from the stands. So moments before Florida took on Vandy in the SEC showdown in Nashville, the public-address announcer pleaded with "the greatest fans in the world" not to throw anything onto the floor. Apparently, not everyone was listening.

Florida needed the victory to stay even with the Commodores in the conference standings. But as the final seconds in regulation time ticked away, it looked like the Gators were about to fall.

With six seconds left to play and trailing Vandy 72–70, Florida had one last chance, but a long pass by Livingston Chatman sailed out of bounds and the ball went over to Vanderbilt. The clock showed only one second left.

All the Commodores had to do was inbound the ball to win the game.

All the Vandy fans had to do was sit on their tennis balls for one more second.

Neither happened.

Elated over the turnover, the fans launched a fusillade of tennis balls at Schintzius one second too soon. The bright yellow balls peppered the 7-foot, 2-inch center, while Coach Newton raced onto the court frantically waving his arms and pleading with the fans to stop. It's an automatic technical foul on the home team if the crowd throws things onto the court during the game.

But Newton's efforts were too late. The instant the first tennis ball hit the floor and before Vandy could inbound the ball, John Clougherty—one of the SEC's most respected referees—immediately signaled for a two-shot technical foul.

With Newton vehemently arguing the call, Schintzius stepped to the charity stripe. As 15,498 fans screamed and hollered, the Gator calmly sank both foul shots to tie the score and send the game into overtime.

For Schintzius, revenge was so sweet. In the overtime he hit seven straight points before Vanderbilt could score as he paced Florida to a critical 81–78 win.

What should have been a hard-fought victory for the Commodores turned into a stunning overtime loss. They never recovered from the blow. Florida went on to win the SEC championship with a 13–5 record, while Vandy finished tied for second place with Alabama at 12–6.

"I've had some tough times playing here, and this is kind of a payback," said Schintzius after the game. "It was a costly mistake by the fans and really kind of dumb. Vandy had the game won until the tennis balls hit the floor. Whoever was stupid enough to do that and say, 'I hit Dwayne Schintzius with a tennis ball,' can now say, 'I cost Vanderbilt the game.' I hope they're happy.

"I don't know who did it, but Dwayne Schintzius thanks you very much!"

MISS THUNDER THIGHS AND
APRIL THE FLASHER

Jacksonville University ○ Dec. 17, 1985

To distract opposing teams' free throw shooters, Jacksonville University students tried to gross them out by holding up a giant poster of a fat lady in a bikini. As if that weren't diabolical enough, the students recruited a real-life sexy model to flash the enemy players.

Ed Radloff and his fellow Phi Gamma Delta fraternity brothers—known on campus as the Fijis—were unhappy over the JU Dolphins' lackluster performances and the apathy of fellow students. "The games were boring, the team was terrible, and the cheerleaders shuffled around like zombies," said Radloff. "People just sat around on their hands. We wanted to stir up some excitement."

Early in the 1985–86 season, a frat brother came home with a poster-sized photograph that grossed out everyone who had ever admired a stuffed bikini. The poster girl was a 350-pound behemoth

Jon Peters/Jacksonville University

attired in a teeny bikini that could hardly be seen under her flabby folds of fat.

One look at the poster and Radloff had a brainstorm. "It was perfect," he said. "I figured if it was outrageous enough to shock a bunch of guys sitting around the kind of animal house we lived in, then just imagine the effect it would have if we stuck it in front of a player in the middle of a basketball game."

At the next home game, the Fijis sat in the first row of seats behind the opposition's basket at the Jacksonville Coliseum. The first time an opposing player came to the line for a free throw, the frat boys grandly unfurled Miss Thunder Thighs in all her glorious tonnage.

It worked perfectly. Radloff shook the poster, the Fijis hurled insults, and the distracted player missed the shot while the crowd cheered wildly.

With her amazing ability to rattle a free throw shooter, the Fiji Fatty became a fixture at home games. The poster was encased in a sturdy, eye-catching frame to ensure that Miss Thunder Thighs got maximum exposure. There was no way a player at the charity stripe could concentrate totally on making the shot—not when he was confronted with the enlarged photo of the obese femme fatale and taunted with such catcalls as "Yo! It's your mama!"

According to the Fijis' informal statistics, the free throw shooting percentage dropped from about 75 percent to around 50 percent whenever Miss Thunder Thighs appeared. "Once we got a player's attention, he was ours for the rest of the game," gloated Radloff.

Just before Christmas the nationally ranked North Carolina Tar Heels came to town. In the spirit of the season, the Fijis jazzed up Miss Thunder Thighs' poster with a string of blinking Christmas tree lights attached to the frame. The frat boys rounded up a supply of extension cords and strung them together in a long line that ran through the stands to the nearest outlet in the Coliseum lobby.

But the Fijis decided that Miss T.T. couldn't carry the load of such a big game all alone. So they recruited a real live looker—April the Flasher. April was a tall, sexy aspiring model whom one of the Fijis had met at a sandwich shop. When she heard that ESPN was televising the game and that her attributes would be seen nationwide, April happily agreed to flash the Tar Heels.

She arrived for the game wearing a trench coat that covered a bright red, French-style swimsuit that was cut skimpy enough to make a nudist blush.

"They made a stunning pair," said Radloff. "Everything April didn't have, Miss Thunder Thighs had in abundance. Or should that be the other way around?"

The Fijis kept April under wraps throughout the first half. They stuck with Miss T.T., whose fat form loused up the form of North Carolina's free throw shooters. The Tar Heels, who entered the game averaging 75.3 percent from the line, went 0-for-4 in the first half with its free throw shooters staring at the fat lady.

April the Flasher didn't show her stuff until 17:10 left to play in the game with the Dolphins surprisingly ahead, 45–41. North Carolina's Kenny Smith had just been fouled and was at the line. But Radloff, Miss Thunder Thighs, and April the Flasher happened to be at the wrong end of the court. With JU students cheering them on, Radloff grabbed the model and the poster and raced around the court to get in position. By the time they arrived, Smith had already sunk the first of a one-and-one.

Before Smith could get the second shot off, Radloff stood beneath the basket and hoisted the electrified and disgusting Miss Thunder Thighs high above his head. Meanwhile, April the Flasher stood in front of the poster, opening and closing her trench coat in classic flasher style, while undulating her scantily clad body.

Predictably, Smith missed the second shot.

However, the Fijis' antics attracted another Smith's attention—Dean Smith, coach of the Tar Heels. The coach complained to the officials about the distraction, but referee John Moreau was already taking steps to end the burlesque.

Jacksonville athletic director Paul Griffin and JU coach Bob Wenzel were summoned to the scorer's table and warned that if the fatty and the flasher were seen again under similar conditions, the Dolphins would be assessed a technical foul.

Reluctantly, Griffin ordered Radloff and his female friends to chill out for the rest of the game. "Personally," Griffin said, "I think the kids were just out to have a good time. They weren't trying to be obnoxious. My only objection was that they were right on the edge of the court."

Without further diversions from Miss Thunder Thighs and April the Flasher, the Tar Heels pulled ahead and won the game in a squeaker, 69–65.

Afterward, April the Flasher dropped from sight, but Radloff, now an alumnus, still takes Miss Thunder Thighs to an occasional Dolphins game. "People expect me to show up with her, but the university doesn't like it," he said. "So now it's more guerrilla warfare than a frontal attack. I have to sneak her in."

SYRACUSE NATIONALS FANS

State Fair Coliseum ○ 1948–64

Rabid Syracuse Nationals fans turned the State Fair Coliseum into a snake pit for opposing teams—by harassing players with hairpin stabbings, leg-hair pulling, and choking cigar smoke.

The Coliseum, where the Nats played their home games, "was a terrible joint for basketball," recalled Art Deutsch, former Syracuse general manager. The court was surrounded by a track that usually was reserved for the numerous horse shows that were held there. But when the Nats played, the track became a convenient standing-room-only area for fans who pushed into the narrow space by the thousands.

The actual seating capacity in the Coliseum was only about 4,200, but raucous mobs of 8,000 to 9,000 were often shoehorned into the place, so the pack on the track often outnumbered the fans in the stands.

Because the standees were jammed in so close to the action on the court, the fans often took a personal hand in the scoring. For example, both baskets were supported by portable stanchions. In close games, with the opposition trying to score, Syracuse fans weren't above shaking the supports to deflect the shot.

The State Fair Coliseum was known for its hatpin ladies and leg-hair pullers—those fans who crowded at courtside and made life miserable for any rival player forced to inbound a ball in their territory.

When an opposing player stood out of bounds, he risked getting jabbed in the back of the leg with a hat pin, usually by a sly young woman projecting an air of innocence. There wasn't much a player could do about getting stabbed. Even to attempt to reprimand such a demure young thing would have brought the wrath of Syracuse down upon him.

The Coliseum's hair pullers were another matter. "There wasn't much room between us players and the fans, so they would reach out and pull the hair on our legs," recalled Hall of Famer Slater Martin, who played for the Minneapolis Lakers and St. Louis Hawks.

"But there was always a cure for things like that. The next time down the court, you'd have a teammate stand in front of the guy [hair puller]. Then the player would move away quickly and you'd hit the guy with the ball right in the face. You wouldn't have to worry about him anymore."

In the Coliseum, with its already poor ventilation, Nats fans connived an ingenious scheme to rattle the opposition, mainly George Mikan of the 1951–52 world champion Lakers and the game's first superstar.

Following an earlier trip to the Coliseum, Mikan made the mistake of complaining publicly that the arena was too smoky from fans' cigarettes and that it bothered him.

"The next time we went to Syracuse," recalled Mikan's teammate Vern Mikkelsen, "it seemed like everybody in the place was puffing on a smelly old stogie. By the third quarter there were layers of smoke hanging over the floor. We had to peek between layers just to find our way downcourt."

Paul Seymour, who spent 13 seasons at Syracuse as a player and player-coach, said the Nats had their own problems with the smoky atmosphere in the Coliseum.

"We had basically an outside shooting team," Seymour said. "The big joke was that if you shot the ball too high you wouldn't see it until it came back down through the thick layer of smoke."

Bud Vander Veer, who covered the Nats' games as a sportswriter, also recalled how the smoke was always a factor that gave the Coliseum its special air.

"Benches for both teams were behind the basket on one end of the floor and the press facilities were on the other end," said Vander Veer. "Sometimes the smoke was so thick that it was difficult to follow the action at the opposite end of the court. Fans who sat in the upper rows of seats just had to guess what was going on down below."

OFFENDING OFFICIALS

Sometimes the outcomes of games aren't decided by the actions of the players, the decisions of the coaches, or the calls by the referees. Sometimes they are decided by the people sitting behind a courtside table—the official scorer and the official timekeeper. Sometimes the games are tipped one way or the other because these officials screwed up. For "The Worst Mistakes by Scorekeepers and Timekeepers," The Basketball Hall of SHAME inducts the following:

BASKETBALL OFFICIALS
Munich Olympic Games ○ Sept. 10, 1972

In the worst miscarriage of justice in basketball history, not to mention Olympic history, bumbling referees and a power-crazed courtside official cheated the U.S. basketball team out of the gold medal it rightfully had won.

The Americans had beaten the Soviet squad in regulation time, but, astoundingly, officials gave the Russians two more opportunities to win. On the third—and illegal—try, the Soviets scored a last-second basket for an unbelievable 51–50 gold medal victory in the 1972 Games in Munich. It was the first defeat for an American Olympic basketball team that had won 62 straight games since the sport first became an Olympic event in 1936.

In the final game against the Russians, the United States staged a valiant rally and trailed 49–48 when American Doug Collins picked up a loose ball at midcourt, drove for the basket, and was fouled with only three seconds left to play. Despite the crushing pressure, the Illinois State senior calmly sank both free throws to give the United States a dramatic 50–49 lead.

But then the officials stole the victory—and the gold medal—from the Americans when the Soviets were given three opportunities to score the winning basket.

The clock showed three seconds remaining when the Soviets inbounded the ball and it was deflected at midcourt. A crowd rushed onto the floor thinking the Americans had won. But referee Renato Righetto of Brazil blew his whistle when he saw the Russian coaches converge on the scorers' table, demanding a time-out. Two seconds had elapsed and the official clock showed one second remaining.

At this point, Great Britain's Dr. R. William Jones intervened. Jones, secretary-general of the International Amateur Basketball Federation (FIBA), ordered the clock set back to three seconds. Jones acted illegally because he had no right to make any rulings during a game; only the referees could do that. Nevertheless, Jones ruled FIBA with an iron hand, and no one dared question his authority.

For the second time the Soviet team took the ball out of bounds, but Modestas Paulauskas' desperation shot was short. The horn sounded and the American players joined the crowd at midcourt, jubilant over their comeback and apparent victory. But their happiness was short-lived.

The clock had not been reset, and Jones, wielding power he didn't legally possess, ordered three seconds—not one second—again posted on the clock. Then he informed both coaches that the Soviet team would have one last play.

Hank Iba, the U.S. coach who had led American teams to gold medals in 1964 and 1968, angrily stalked after Jones and the referees and had to be restrained by his players before play began again.

The Soviet team made the most of its third chance to score. Tom McMillen, the 6-foot, 11-inch forward from Maryland, waved his arms to thwart the inbounds pass as he had done on the previous two attempts, but this time the referee ordered him to back off. When he did, Soviet player Ivan Yedeshko backed up, wound up, and threw the ball the length of the court to 6-foot, 8-inch Aleksander Belov. Americans Kevin Joyce and Robert Forbes went up for the ball with Belov, but he knocked them off-balance with an obvious foul that wasn't called and then easily sank the ball one second before time expired for an incredible 51–50 Soviet victory.

Chaos ensued. Iba again rushed the scorers' table, Forbes wept unabashedly, and newsmen and irate fans flooded onto the floor. "I've never seen anything like this in all my years of basketball," Iba declared.

In the wild closing seconds, the referees neglected to call two violations that were evident in the game films. One showed that

Yedeshko had stepped on the baseline in making his full-court pass to Belov, which would have negated the scoring play and given the ball to the Americans.

The second oversight was equally flagrant—not calling a three-second violation against Belov. Under international rules, the three-second rule goes into effect once the official gives the ball to the player out of bounds, not when the clock begins. The refs failed to notice that Belov had stationed himself inside the three-second lane for at least five seconds.

The official result of the game was delayed because Hank Iba filed a protest that was considered by a five-man FIBA jury of appeals made up of members from Cuba, Poland, Puerto Rico, Hungary, and Italy. It was a kangaroo court because the members from the three Soviet-bloc nations—Cuba, Poland, and Hungary—naturally upheld the Russians' victory, while the minority—the Italian and Puerto Rican representatives—voted to disallow Belov's basket.

The U.S. team had a vote of their own—they decided unanimously to refuse their silver medals because they had been robbed of their victory.

Hank Iba was doubly victimized. First, he was fleeced out of the gold medal. Then, while he was arguing with officials at courtside after the game, Iba's wallet with $370 was filched. "They've even taken to picking my pockets," the coach lamented in the locker room. "What else can go wrong?"

BILL GILLESPIE

Notre Dame Scorekeeper

JOHNNY GLENN

Northwestern Scorekeeper

Dec. 31, 1935

In the greatest scorekeeping blunder in hoops history, the officials keeping the game book both lost track of the scoring at the same time.

As a result, the Northwestern Wildcats' apparent 20–19 victory over the Notre Dame Fighting Irish turned into the only tie basketball game in major college competition.

The double-headed blunder occurred late in the second half of the annual New Year's Eve clash between the neighboring universities. Each school recruited a student manager to act as a co-official scorer for the game, which was played at Northwestern's Patten Gym.

With the scoreboard reading Notre Dame 16, Northwestern 13

late in the second half, Irish forward Ray Meyer was fouled and sank the free throw. Minutes later Meyer was fouled again and also converted that charity toss—which was witnessed by six sportswriters covering the game and the 5,800 spectators in the stands.

However, scorekeepers Bill Gillespie and Johnny Glenn never marked down the successful free throw in either game book. The scoreboard wrongly read Notre Dame 17, Northwestern 13 instead of 18–13. The Wildcats then made two quick field goals and a free throw. The scoreboard now had Northwestern leading 18–17 when the score should have been deadlocked at 18–18.

With two minutes to go, the Wildcats sank another basket for their 20th point. Then, with less than ten seconds to play, Notre Dame star Johnny Ford drilled a long-range basket that the fans in the stands and the sportswriters thought for sure had tied the game.

But the final score read Northwestern 20, Notre Dame 19. Both teams, unaware of the scorekeepers' gaffe, left the court. Gillespie and Glenn prepared to pack up and go home. Meanwhile, the reporters and fans—knowing the scoreboard was wrong and assuming the players did too—sat around waiting for the expected overtime period to start.

When word spread that the players were unaware of the tie and were taking their showers, the sportswriters launched their own protest. They had been keeping their own tally sheets, which didn't jibe with the official scoring. They quickly found the error. Neither Gillespie nor Glenn had any record of Meyer's second free throw.

The referees, Nick Kearns and Lyle Clarno, refused to be drawn into the controversy. "I don't know what the score is," grumped Kearns. "That's the scorekeepers' job."

By the time the confused officials recognized their error and corrected the scoring to reflect the 20–20 deadlock, it was too late to get the teams back on the court for an overtime period.

Notre Dame coach George Keogan was eager for a rematch. "The game obviously was a tie," argued Keogan. "The only fair thing to do is play it over. Notre Dame is willing to meet Northwestern any time and any place."

Not until the next day did Northwestern concede that the game had ended in a tie. But because the Wildcats' schedule was full, the game was never replayed. "Just call this game a tie and mark it down as another manifestation of the intense rivalry between Notre Dame and Northwestern," said Wildcats athletic director K. L. Wilson.

While the Wildcats–Fighting Irish foul-up was the first such tie game between two major colleges, there was at least one earlier incident.

On Feb. 9, 1918, fans and players were under the impression that Kentucky Wesleyan had beaten Kentucky 21–20. But after both teams had left the gym, a recount of the record book revealed the final score was actually 21–21. No one ever solved the mystery of Kentucky's missing point. The game was never replayed.

BOB BILLINGS
Timekeeper

RONNIE NUNN
Referee

Jan. 15, 1990

Timekeeper Bob Billings and referee Ronnie Nunn let the New York Knicks steal a game from the Chicago Bulls in a fraction of a second.

It takes longer to say "tenth of a second" than it does for that amount of time to pass. Yet, according to the two officials, it took less time than that for the Knicks' Trent Tucker to catch an inbounds pass, turn around, jump, aim, and swish a game-winning three pointer from 26 feet away.

The Bulls, the Knicks, the partisan Madison Square Garden fans, and even NBA Commissioner David Stern, who was watching from courtside, knew it was humanly impossible to do all that in a tenth of a second. But the impossible goal counted and the Knicks won 109–106.

However, the Bulls refused to believe their eyes. They later filed a protest arguing that Tucker wasn't Superman and couldn't move at the speed of light. The play consumed closer to two seconds, the Bulls insisted, meaning the game should have gone into overtime instead of into the Knicks' win column.

The Bulls' protest was rejected and the Knicks' tainted victory went into the record book.

The incident was the first controversy involving the international clock that displays tenths of a second during the last minute of each quarter. The NBA began using the system in the 1989–90 season and found that the players and coaches liked knowing exactly how much time is left.

In the Knicks' "Beat the Clock" game, New York and Chicago were knotted up 106–106 with 0.1 second showing on the game clock. With possession of the ball on their side of the court, the

Knicks called time-out and designed a "Hail Mary" play—even though they knew in their hearts there wasn't enough time left to pull it off.

Over in the Bulls' huddle, Phil Jackson was already thinking overtime. He told his team that the only way the Knicks could win in regulation was on a one-in-a-million chance that New York center Patrick Ewing could tap in an alley-oop pass. The Bulls set their defense to prevent such a long shot.

Knicks coach Stu Jackson had the same idea. "We wanted to run Trent along the baseline as a decoy and then lob the ball to Patrick," he said. "What happened was that as Trent was coming off the screen on Patrick, [Chicago guard] Michael Jordan stopped to take the lob away. It was not the shot we wanted but Trent was open and he turned around and hit the prayer."

But the Knicks needed more than a prayer. They needed a reinterpretation of the laws of physics. And they got it.

As the Knicks set up the final play, Nunn waited to signal Billings when to start the clock. Mark Jackson then inbounded the ball to Tucker. Now here's where science and officiating don't jibe. From Nunn's eyes to his brain to his hand signaling the clock to start . . . and from Billings' eyes to his brain to his hand flipping the switch . . . and from the toggle switch to the inner workings of the clock to the horn, somehow all that consumed less than one-tenth of an official second. In the meantime, Tucker had time to toss up his prayer.

Both officials maintained they were right. Billings insisted he flipped his switch properly. "Just when everybody gets used to the tenth of a second, they'll probably go to one-hundredths," he added.

"I turned and looked and the shot was released in time," said Nunn.

But at least one NBA honcho disagreed. Before the protest was denied, Rod Thorn, the league's vice president of operations, said it was ". . . physically impossible to catch a ball and shoot it in one-tenth of a second. The officials should not have counted the shot. I hate to say it, but the officials made a mistake."

Thorn added that in Europe, where the clock has measured tenths of a second for years, tests have shown that it takes at least three-tenths of a second just to have an inbounds pass touch a player and then go back out of bounds.

Phil Jackson wasn't too shocked over the cockeyed clock controversy. As a player with the Knicks during the 1970s, he often benefited from the bizarre clock in the Garden that mysteriously ran slow when the Knicks were behind but speeded up when the home team was ahead.

"You can't get off a shot in one-tenth of a second," Jackson concluded. "But this is Madison Square Garden, and I was here a long time and that's all I have to say."

But Knicks guard Gerald Wilkins had more to say even if Jackson didn't. "That's the advantage of playing at home," chortled Wilkins. "Sometimes the guy running the clock can be in a daze."

MUGGSIE MASON

Scorekeeper ○ Cleveland State Vikings ○ Feb. 8, 1983

The Cleveland State Vikings beat the Akron University Zips 82–82. No, that's not a typo. That was the *real* score. However, the *official* score was 83–82, because scorekeeper Muggsie Mason somehow gave the winners an extra phantom point.

"It was just a plain old screwup," admitted Merle Levin, Cleveland State's sports information director. "We're still trying to live it down— but we'll take the win any way we can get it."

The favored Zips (12–7) were trailing the Vikings (6–16) 38–32 at Cleveland's Public Hall when Akron took a 40–38 lead on a basket by Tim Spikes. But the scoreboard suddenly showed the score as 40–39.

Incredibly, no one on the Akron bench noticed Cleveland's unearned extra point. And so, at halftime, the Zips were ahead only 49–43 instead of 49–42.

At least some people suspected something was wrong. *Akron Beacon Journal* sportswriter Bob Nold, who was covering the game, spotted the error. The announcers broadcasting the game over WAKR radio claimed later they thought the score was wrong. But no one said anything at the time.

That's because they were misled by the play-by-play sheets distributed to the press table at halftime. Mysteriously, Cleveland State's 38 was scratched out and a 39 was written in. To account for the phantom point, Vikings forward Dave Schultz's free throw figures— which were really 3-for-4—were changed to 4-for-5.

"Clearly this is a case for Agatha Christie's ace, Hercule Poirot," wrote Nold in the *Beacon Journal*. "It would appear . . . the scoring [had] been changed to match the scoreboard instead of vice versa."

When questioned later about the discrepancy, Muggsie Mason, who had been Cleveland State's official scorekeeper for years, had no explanation for the phantom point.

Ken McDonald, Akron's sports information director at the time, said he was keeping the scorebook for the Zips and let Mason's scoring error slip right by him. "It was just one of those things that got by everybody," said McDonald. "Usually I check the book at the half, but Coach [Bob] Rupert wanted it. We came back late for the second half, so I just wrote down what was in the official scorebook."

Apparently everyone else who was puzzled by the score did the same thing. They quietly changed their own score sheets to reflect Mason's botched version.

At the time, it didn't seem to matter much. The Zips were coasting in the second half and several times enjoyed leads of ten points. They still led 80–73 with 2:30 to play. But then they let down defensively. The Vikings stormed back and won the game on a desperation shot that was in the air when the final buzzer sounded.

The dramatic bucket should have sent the game into overtime. Instead, it sent the Zips home with a bizarre 82–82 defeat.

"I didn't realize there was an error until we were on the bus home," said McDonald. "In 20 years, that's the first time I've seen anything like this ever happen."

The general feeling of most of the players on the Akron team—which didn't protest the game—was summed up best by a Zip who said, "Maybe we did deserve to lose—but not by 82–82."

LARRY BATES

Timekeeper
March 21, 1986

DALE HOFFPAUIR

Timekeeper
March 23, 1990

Twice in four years, the Michigan State Spartans missed making it to the Final Four when they ran afoul of fouled-up time clocks and timekeepers.

"I'm beginning to think we're snakebit," said Michigan State coach Jud Heathcote. "We can beat the teams we play, but we seem to have trouble beating the clock."

The first time the Spartans were victimized by basketball's version of the Long Count—or what Heathcote calls "home clockin' "—was during the semifinal game of the Midwest Regionals in 1986. Michigan State was playing Kansas in Kansas City's Kemper Arena, just a few miles down the pike from the Jayhawks' campus.

With the clock showing 2:21 left in the game, Vernon Carr's free throw gave Michigan State a four-point lead, 76–72. But after the Jayhawks moved downcourt, passed the ball around several times, and scored on a tip-in, the clock showed only one second having elapsed.

Meanwhile, Heathcote, quick to spot the lazy clock, was up and pounding on the scorer's table to draw attention to the obvious malfunction. The coach pleaded his case to official timekeeper Larry Bates.

Heathcote had good reason to complain. The official play-by-plays kept on a computer showed that 12 seconds had elapsed while time stood still on the game clock. Technicians for CBS, which was televising the game, counted 15 seconds. Most observers agreed that the clock hadn't moved for at least 10 seconds. However, despite the coach's protests, the obvious mistake was not corrected.

The timing error played a critical role in the game. Those extra seconds gave the Jayhawks just enough time to tie the game on a basket with only nine seconds remaining. Kansas then beat Michigan State in overtime, 96–86.

"If those ten seconds had gone off the clock like they should have," thundered Heathcote, "the game would have been over before they tied it."

Arnie Ferrin, a member of the tournament committee, shrugged off Heathcote's argument that the error should have been corrected. Technically, Ferrin admitted, Bates, the timekeeper, should have informed the officials on the floor that the clock wasn't working properly at the change of possession following Carr's free throw.

"He probably could have blown the horn, called the officials, and said, 'I don't know how much time was lost,' " added Ferrin. "There could have been a conference with the coaches over how much time to take off the clock, but that didn't happen, so there was nothing we could do about it."

The Spartans lost the argument, lost the game, and lost their shot at the Final Four. When it was over, even Kansas coach Larry Brown, who profited most from the lost seconds, sympathized with Heathcote's plight. "I think the fact that there was a malfunction ruined the whole night," said Brown.

In 1990 the Spartans experienced an eerie sense of déjà vu when they were again counted out of contention by both the clock and a blown timing call during the semifinal game in the Southeast Regional played in New Orleans.

Michigan State seemed to have the game won when they went ahead of the Georgia Tech Yellow Jackets 75–73 with only five seconds left and Spartans guard Steve Smith at the free throw line shooting a one-and-one.

But Smith missed the first shot and Tech came down with the rebound. Tech's Johnny McNeil fired the ball out to guard Kenny Anderson, who almost lost the ball at midcourt before dribbling to the top of the key and nailing a desperation jumper from the three-point line at the buzzer.

Referee John Clougherty signaled that the three-pointer counted, which would have given the Yellow Jackets the win. But another official, Charles Range, said Anderson's foot was on the line. After a conference, the officials ruled that Anderson's jumper was a two-pointer that tied the game.

But an emotional Heathcote didn't care whether the basket was two or three points. He argued that it should be no points since time had expired before Anderson had even launched his shot.

In fact, a frame-by-frame replay of the play on CBS clearly showed the ball was still in Anderson's hands when the clock read 0:00.

But official timer Dale Hoffpauir rejected Heathcote's pleas for a television replay to settle the controversy since the NCAA allows such replays only in the case of clock malfunctions or fights.

Roy Kramer, the Southeastern Conference commissioner and a member of the tournament committee, added, "You don't watch the clock to determine whether the shot is good or not. The official has got to watch the line and watch the shot."

Even after Kramer had viewed the replay, he still hemmed and hawed over the blown call. "It's a judgment call," Kramer said. "The game is officiated by human beings. It's not officiated by electronic machines."

When officials ruled that the game was tied at 75–75 and ordered the overtime period to continue, Heathcote was resigned to a bad outcome.

He was right. Georgia Tech won 81–80.

TRAVELING TRAVESTIES

Some of the most horrendous moments for teams don't happen on the court; they happen on the road. Just getting to the game can be more difficult than playing it. With some of the wild misadventures teams have faced while traveling, they know firsthand what Dorothy meant when she said, "There's no place like home." For "The Most Dreadful Road Trips," The Basketball Hall of SHAME inducts the following:

JACKSONVILLE UNIVERSITY DOLPHINS

Feb. 22–26, 1982

A five-day, two-game road trip turned into the "Voyage of the Damned" for the Jacksonville University Dolphins.

Not one but two airlines lost their luggage and equipment, forcing the Dolphins to practice in street clothes and run drills with imaginary basketballs.

The team left the warm confines of their Florida school on a Tuesday en route to the much colder Richmond for a Wednesday night game against Virginia Commonwealth.

However, ice on the runway knocked out the landing lights at Richmond, and the flight was rerouted to Atlanta. After a long delay the Dolphins caught a flight to Norfolk, boarded a bus with no heater, and spent the next three and a half hours riding through the subfreezing night to reach Richmond.

Once there, however, the team learned its luggage had stayed behind in Atlanta. Coach Bob Wenzel was forced to conduct practice the next day with players in street clothes. Luckily, the uniforms arrived by game time. Unluckily, the Dolphins were hammered by their unsympathetic hosts 94–68.

On Thursday morning, the team faced another travel travesty. On their way to Mobile to play South Alabama, they changed planes in Greenville, South Carolina, and arrived on schedule at their Mobile hotel. But because of a mixup, they had to wait 90 minutes before they could check in—which really didn't matter since their luggage had been accidentally left behind by the airline in Greenville.

Their baggage finally showed up the following day. The Dolphins then went to the Mobile Municipal Auditorium for an afternoon workout. But their equipment bags had been misplaced and no basketballs were available.

To his credit, Wenzel persevered. He ordered his squad to practice anyway. So for 20 wacky minutes, the team ran through full-court drills with imaginary basketballs!

"There were a lot of fabulous reverse dunks and some fancy passing like you'd expect to find in an NBA all-star game," said Wenzel. "But it kept the kids from focusing on the fact that they were in the middle of a disaster."

Despite their tribulations, the Dolphins later that night upset favored South Alabama 95–91 in overtime.

"There was some talk afterwards about continuing to practice without a ball, but I felt we'd pushed our luck about as far as we could," recalled Wenzel.

"I was just happy to get home. It was a real 'Voyage of the Damned.'"

UNINTENTIONAL CONTACT(S)

DePauw University player Kevin Golden lost sight of an upcoming game at Dayton University.

The night before the 1986 game, Golden put his contact lenses in a glass of water next to his hotel bed. The next morning, his contacts were gone.

Golden soon discovered why. His roommate, Andy Laux, had awakened thirsty in the middle of the night, seen the glass by the bed, and unwittingly slurped the contacts down with the water.

UNIVERSITY OF WASHINGTON HUSKIES

Jan. 3–5, 1990

The Washington Huskies set out for a couple of routine games in Arizona and wound up in the Twilight Zone.

For bizarre road trips, nothing matched the shameful misadventures the Huskies experienced as they wandered through the Arizona wilderness in search of an exit.

The road trip started badly even before the Huskies got out of Seattle. The team's flight was delayed and the players sat around the airport while arrangements were made with another airline to get the squad to Tucson to play the University of Arizona.

"I wanted to arrive early enough so the team could rest up and get in a good practice," explained Coach Lynn Nance. "But the plane was late and things just went downhill after that."

In fact, things went downhill like an avalanche. When the Huskies finally arrived in Tucson, the bus that was supposed to meet them was nowhere in sight. After searching in vain for their transportation, Nance finally rounded up enough taxicabs to get his tired players to the hotel.

Meanwhile, the missing bus and driver were located—120 miles away parked at the Phoenix airport, waiting for the Huskies to show up there.

Early the next morning, the bus driver left for Tucson to collect the Huskies and deliver them to the Arizona State campus in Tempe where they were scheduled to play the Sun Devils.

En route to Tucson, the driver was stopped on Interstate 10 for speeding 85 mph in a 55-mph zone. The highway patrol officer wrote an additional citation when he discovered the bus driver didn't have the required log book. Then the cop ordered the bus out of service when he spotted a badly worn front tire.

The officer followed the bus to a nearby truck stop. But instead of replacing the tire, the driver continued on to Tucson as soon as the cop was out of sight.

The next day the Washington team, still smarting from a 65–51 loss to the Arizona Wildcats the night before, piled into the bus for the drive to Tempe. But Nance noticed that the 100-mile trip seemed to take forever.

"I was sitting behind the driver," recalled Nance. "We were barely moving and just when I leaned over to ask what the speed limit was, the driver whipped off the interstate and started to double back."

The addled driver had missed a mandatory inspection stop for commercial vehicles and had ducked off the main highway hoping to avoid detection.

"But how the hell do you hide a bus?" Nance asked. "Besides, it was too late. A red light and siren came on behind us and the driver pulled over. I asked him if he had been speeding and the guy replied, 'No, but I'm in big trouble.'"

Bigger than he imagined. The cop was the same one who had stopped the bus driver the day before. This time there were no tickets and no warnings. The burly officer boarded the bus, arrested the driver, and led him away in handcuffs. Other squad cars arrived on the scene to assist in the arrest.

"I thought we were being driven by some dangerous fugitive," Nance said. "And there we were stuck out in the middle of the desert with no driver and a bus the police wouldn't allow back on the highway."

Nance pleaded his case with the patrolmen. They agreed to drive Nance and his assistants back to Tucson to rent minivans and get the team to Tempe in time for the game.

Meanwhile, one of the cops on the scene was bitten by another K-9 officer's dog and had to seek treatment. "I guess our bad luck was starting to rub off," Nance joked.

But there was more bad luck to come. The Huskies lost again to Arizona State 63–48. Sighed Nance, "After all that happened on the trip, I wasn't surprised."

GENE CONLEY

Center ○ New York Knicks ○ Dec. 18, 1963

Gene Conley wanted to "bomb" his former Boston Celtics teammates. Unfortunately, he announced his intentions while boarding a plane— and he was quickly grounded by the FBI.

"It was really a dumb move," recalled the colorful Conley. "I shot off my mouth at the wrong time and in the wrong place—and it almost landed me in jail."

Conley, one of the few athletes who played two pro sports, spent most of his career in Bean Town playing for both the Celtics and the Red Sox. When the big center was traded to the New York Knicks, he still kept his home in Boston and commuted to and from New York throughout the basketball season.

UPI/Bettmann

"It only cost about $15 to take the shuttle flight between New York and Boston, so it was cheaper for me to fly back and forth than move to New York," Conley explained. "Since I was flying so much, the people at the airport gate got to know me, and we were always kidding around."

But Conley went one joke too far when he prepared to board a flight from New York to Boston the night before the Knicks were to play the Celtics in the Boston Garden.

"The guys at the gate knew I had played for Boston," said Conley. "One of them teased me about having to go home to play the tough Celtics. I just laughed and yelled back, 'Oh, yeah? Well, we're going to bomb the hell out of 'em.' "

Conley went on board and took his usual seat at the rear of the plane. But the flight failed to leave on schedule.

"We sat there for a long time and I couldn't figure out why we weren't taking off," Conley continued. "Pretty soon these two guys in suits got on and started down the aisle asking questions. People kept pointing back to where I was sitting.

"When the guys got to me, one of them asked if I was a basketball player. There I sat, all six feet, eight inches of me, with my little Knicks bag on my lap and wearing my Knicks jacket, and this guy wants to know if I'm a basketball player. It was pretty obvious I wasn't a jockey.

"Then they asked if I had made the comment about bombing something. I figured they were disgruntled Celtics fans, so I said 'sure.' That's when they flashed their FBI badges in my face and ordered me off the plane."

With the planeload of passengers watching nervously, the G-men marched Conley up the aisle, escorted him to an airport security office, and grilled him for hours.

Unfortunately, Conley's "bomb 'em" comment had been over-heard by a fellow passenger who took him seriously and reported the "threat."

Long after his flight had taken off, Conley finally convinced the agents that he really was who he claimed to be and that "bombing" Boston was part of his job.

"There had been a lot of hijackings and bomb threats about that time," recalled Conley. "The agents warned me not to make any more remarks like that even if I was just kidding. It shook me up because there was jail time and a $5,000 fine for making real bomb threats.

"Just before they released me, those guys had the nerve to hit me up for a couple of tickets to a Knicks game. So much for the great Untouchables!"

Conley had to catch a later flight. And just to rub salt in the wound, the Celtics ended up bombing Conley and the Knicks 133–111.

UNIVERSITY OF TENNESSEE VOLUNTEERS

Feb. 20, 1952

A routine road trip to play the Georgia Tech Yellow Jackets in Atlanta turned into a wild misadventure for the Tennessee Volunteers.

Before they ever stepped foot on the court, the Vols had to contend with firemen and policemen, jail and bail. Adding to their woes, all the excitement triggered an asthma attack in a key player. Then, to top it off, a jammed locker room door trapped the squad inside while the Yellow Jackets cooled their heels on the floor.

The wild pregame ordeal started when Vols forward Ed Wiener dared his roommate, reserve center J. D. Byington, to test the fire alarm system in the Atlanta hotel where the team was resting prior to the game that evening.

Byington took up the challenge, struck a couple of matches by a fire detector, and set off the fire alarm.

"I don't know what they thought they were doing," recalled Tennessee center Herb Neff. "They were just bored, I guess. But they should have known better. Not long before that, there had been a big hotel fire in Atlanta and folks were still pretty nervous about that sort of thing."

They were so nervous, in fact, that seconds after the alarm sounded, the hotel was surrounded by fire trucks, cop cars, and ambulances, all with sirens blaring and red lights flashing.

Dozens of firefighters rushed through the hotel corridors with their axes in hand ready to bust down every door in sight. The automatic sprinklers worked perfectly, soaking the panicky players and guests as they rushed for the exits. Meanwhile, the real culprits cowered in their room while fire inspectors searched each floor.

Wiener and Byington almost escaped detection, but a sharp-eyed fire captain spotted a burned book of matches in their room and started asking them questions.

"At first, the guys denied knowing anything about it," said Neff. "But I think Ed finally admitted what happened."

Byington was hauled away to be charged with setting off a false fire alarm. Coach Emmett Lowery went along, hoping to post his bail. "I had to go to night court, which started about 6 PM, to talk the judge out of putting J. D. behind bars," recalled the coach.

While Lowery was gone, Assistant Coach John Sines gathered the rest of the team and herded them over to Georgia Tech to get ready for the game.

But all the excitement had already taken its toll. Spark-plug guard Joe Treadway, the Vols' best outside shooter, suffered from asthma. The frenzy of the false fire alarm set off an attack so debilitating that Treadway couldn't suit up.

Lowery made it to the arena just minutes before game time and spent a few moments talking to the squad, hoping to settle them down.

"After the coach talked to us, we were ready to go out and play," said Neff. "But when we tried to leave we couldn't get out."

Somehow the door got jammed. Lowery yanked on the knob and kicked the door, but it wouldn't budge. He beat on the door and yelled. The whole squad then pounded on the door and yelled. Finally a maintenance man heard the commotion and freed the Vols just seconds before the scheduled tip-off.

"The coach was pretty upset about the whole sour deal," said Neff. "Lowery was so mad at Ed Wiener and J. D. Byington that they sat on the bench the whole game even though it was a close one and we could have used J. D. But J. D. was so shook up he probably wouldn't have been any good even if the coach had put him in."

Somehow the Volunteers managed to slip past Georgia Tech 83–81. "I sure don't know how we managed to pull it out after all that we went through," said Neff. "The only good thing that happened on that trip was that we won the game—barely. Everything else went to hell."

COPPIN STATE EAGLES

Feb. 26, 1971

BOSTON UNIVERSITY TERRIERS

Dec. 11, 1986

A funny thing happened to the Coppin State Eagles and the Boston University Terriers on their way to games. They both got lost on road trips. Really lost.

The Coppin State squad was so late arriving for their first ever postseason play-off game that the officials had already ordered a forfeit by the time the team showed up. Boston University was an hour overdue for its road game—after going to the wrong university in the wrong city.

In 1971, financially strapped Coppin State finally produced a strong, winning team whose 15–6 record earned an at-large invitation to the NAIA district playoffs.

"Everyone was tremendously excited about making it to a postseason tournament for the first time," recalled Charles Hardnett. He was a former Baltimore Bullets star who acted as the school's part-time coach while he held down another job. "I had to be in Cleveland and couldn't go to the game, and the people who organized the trip didn't have any road experience. It was a miracle they ever got there at all."

Since the school had no budget to charter a bus, team members scrounged up enough cars and drivers to form a caravan for the 275-mile trip from their campus near Baltimore to Mansfield College in northern Pennsylvania. By the time all the cars were lined up and noses were counted, the Eagles were hours late getting on the road. To make matters worse, darkness and fog closed in on them when they reached the Allegheny Mountains.

Meanwhile, at Mansfield College, Mountaineers coach Ed Wilson, his team, and the standing-room-only crowd were getting keyed up for the 8 PM tip-off. "We were all ready to go," said Wilson. "Then we waited and waited and waited. Finally, the tournament officials ordered the game forfeited at 11 PM."

When the Eagles finally found Mansfield College at about midnight, the only reception committee still on hand at the gym was a yawning night watchman. The referees, tournament officials, Mountaineers, and the hometown crowd had given up and gone home hours earlier.

"We learned later that the Coppin State caravan hit fog around Harrisburg," recalled Wilson. "They got separated a couple of times and had to regroup. The lead driver kept getting lost in the fog and all the others just followed right along."

Meanwhile, Hardnett sat in his hotel room in Cleveland anxiously awaiting the outcome of the game. About 2 AM his student assistant called. "He told me the good news was that they only lost by two points," Hardnett said. "The bad news was they never even made it to the game and had to forfeit 2–0.

"It was a terrible experience. Coppin State blew their first big opportunity just because they couldn't find their way to the game."

The Boston University Terriers fared slightly better on their 1986 road-trip odyssey. At least they managed to play—after first going to the wrong school.

The Terriers flew from Boston to Syracuse, New York, en route to a scheduled game against Colgate University. The team piled into a chartered bus at the airport and set out for the Colgate campus located in Hamilton, 35 miles southeast of Syracuse.

Unfortunately, the bus driver headed south*west*.

"The longer we drove the more I was sure we were going in the wrong direction," recalled Boston coach Mike Jarvis. "I kept asking the driver if he knew where he was going. It was like I had insulted the guy. He told me to sit down and stop worrying. He insisted he knew where he was going."

An hour later, the driver triumphantly pulled up in front of the university gymnasium. Jarvis took one look out the window and told the driver, "That's just great. You got us to Cornell, but we're supposed to be at Colgate."

Jarvis called Colgate, told officials there his tale of woe, and convinced them to delay the game. Then the embarrassed driver took the team from the Cornell campus in Ithaca 70 miles to the Colgate campus in Hamilton. What should have been an uneventful 45-minute ride from Syracuse turned into a frustrating two-and-a-half-hour detour.

When the Terriers finally arrived at Colgate, they were so steamed at their wayward bus driver that they took out their anger on Colgate and whipped the Red Raiders 78–65.

PHILADELPHIA 76ERS

Feb. 6–9, 1973

Right in the middle of the worst season in the history of any NBA franchise, the Philadelphia 76ers suffered through one of the league's most dismal road trips.

Even Stephen King couldn't have dreamed up a more horrific scenario than the Awful Sixer Odyssey of '73.

"Looking back," sighed Philly guard Tom Van Arsdale, "it seems like there was kind of a poetic justice to it, because the team was so bad anyway. But at the time it was just a plain nightmare."

The bad dream started when Philadelphia (which finished the season 9–73) lost its 17th straight game to tie the record for consecutive losses. The game with the Houston Rockets was played in San Antonio on a Tuesday night. Since the team didn't have to be in Portland for its next game until Friday night, the Sixers stayed over for some much needed rest in the warm Texas sun.

But the 1972–73 season was a time when everyone was dumping on the downtrodden Sixers—even Mother Nature. On Thursday, the temperature in San Antonio plunged from 72 degrees to a chilling 22 degrees.

The team checked out of its hotel and headed for the airport, but freezing rain moved in and played havoc with the flight schedules as the ice built up. A long neglected de-icing machine was cranked up and sent to thaw out the frozen planes. But the seldom used device clanked to a stop and blew up.

Sorry, the Sixers were told, no planes could take off. The players trudged back to the hotel, only to find their vacated rooms were now occupied. A search turned up rooms in another inn, and the team bedded down late.

On Friday they checked out and drove to the airport. The plane still couldn't leave, so it was back to the hotel. And again the "No Vacancy" sign was out. The despairing 76ers managed to find a third hotel that agreed to take in the vagabonds.

Just as they were checking in, word came that a flight to Portland was about to leave, so back to the airport they dashed. En route, two taxicabs carrying players skidded out of control on the icy streets and crashed. No one was injured, but other cabs had to be dispatched to pick up the stranded players and get them to the plane on time.

Finally, at 4 PM, the Sixers were airborne and bound for an 8 PM tip-off in Portland, 2,095 miles away.

Meanwhile, fans gathered at Memorial Coliseum to await the arrival of the visitors. A bus arrived and a cry of "The Sixers are here!" went up. False alarm. Out stepped a semipro hockey team, unloading gear for a game the next night.

At 9 PM, the crowd was informed the Philadelphia team was in the Coliseum. Another false alarm. The Sixers were still miles away, stuck in a freeway traffic jam.

Eventually the late team made it to the Coliseum. Unfortunately, not all of their luggage did. Some of the players had to borrow jerseys from fellow teammates.

While the Sixers were suiting up, Portland management prepared an announcement telling fans they could exchange their tickets for a future game. But the public address announcer mistakenly informed fans they could get an immediate cash refund. So when the Sixers finally took the court, weary but ready to play, they were greeted with a small-scale riot as fans stampeded to get their money back.

After all that, the game went on. And the Sixers—as expected—

lost number 18 in a row, 116–105, to set a new NBA record. (They lost two more before halting their losing streak.)

"That was the worst day of my life," recalled Van Arsdale, who wore a borrowed jersey. "No, make that the worst two days of my life."

WOEFUL WINDUPS

How could a college team squander an 18-point lead in the final 77 seconds and get beat? How could an NBA squad go scoreless while giving up 19 unanswered points in the final minutes to lose by a single point? How could a top school hold an eight-point lead with just 17 seconds to go—and end up losers? The answer, my friend, is blowin' the win. For "The Most Atrociously Blown Games," The Basketball Hall of SHAME inducts the following:

SHASTA COLLEGE KNIGHTS
Jan. 6, 1990

No college team ever blew a game more shamefully than the Shasta College Knights. That's because they blew the same game not once but twice.

First the team from Redding, California, squandered a huge 18-point lead in the final 77 seconds of regulation time to send the game into overtime. Then the Knights built up an 11-point margin only to fritter it away before finally losing in double overtime.

"It was crazy," said John Abell, coach of the winning Roadrunners of Butte Community College in Oroville, California. "In 30 years of coaching, I've never seen a team collapse the way Shasta did—and I'll probably never see it again."

Shasta, which had led Butte by as much as 26 points in the first half, was coasting along, enjoying a seemingly safe 89–71 advantage with their starters on the bench and just 1:17 left in the game.

But then the Knights turned into the Dazed.

Their shocking collapse began when two Shasta turnovers were sandwiched between two three-pointers and a lay-up by Butte. That sliced the margin to 89–79 with 1:02 left.

Shasta coach Jim Keating rushed his starting lineup back in, but at that point nothing short of inserting the Detroit Pistons' front court would have helped.

Following a Roadrunner free throw and a missed Shasta shot, Butte's 5-foot, 8-inch reserve Scott Joyce hit another three-pointer with 36 seconds left, trimming the deficit to only six. The unnerved Knights turned the ball over again under the pressure of the Roadrunners' full-court press. Then, despite being double-teamed, Joyce scored once more from three-point range. Shasta still led, but only by three, with 29 seconds left. In their panic to hold on, the Knights committed their fifth turnover during the horrifying 77-second run. The ball went back to Joyce, who threw up a desperation 25-footer while falling backward. His third straight three-pointer tied the game at the buzzer.

Somehow the reeling Knights managed to regroup in the first overtime and charged out to an 11-point lead, 103–92, with only 1:54 remaining. But, incredibly, they folded once again. Shasta committed three more turnovers, missed the front end of three one-and-one free throws, and allowed Butte to close within two points, 103–101.

Then with one second remaining, and still leading by the same score, the Knights fouled Nicholas Block while he was in the act of shooting. "Block was a nice kid, but he'd come from a high school team that went 0–52," recalled Abell. "He was our poorest free throw shooter. I knew there was no way he could hit both free throws. But he did. And we tied the game again."

Unbelievably, Shasta had blown its second huge, final-minute lead, allowing Butte to score 11 straight points to send the game into double overtime. There was little doubt who was going to win now. Stunned by their second swoon of the game, the Knights resignedly faced their doom and grimly played out the game. They lost 116–115. As the stunned Shasta players trudged off the floor, the Roadrunners celebrated as if they had won the national championship.

Shasta coach Jim Keating was too shocked to talk to reporters after the game. Even months after the disaster, he was still too embarrassed to return phone calls from The Basketball Hall of SHAME to discuss the collapse.

But Abell wasn't at a loss for words. "I couldn't look at the game film for two weeks," recalled the happy coach. "I was convinced we'd lose if I watched it."

DUKE BLUE DEVILS

March 2, 1974

The Duke Blue Devils played like champs for 39 minutes and 43 seconds. But in the final 17 seconds—when it counted the most—they played like chumps.

That's all the time it took for the red-faced Blue Devils to blow an eight-point lead and lose to the rival North Carolina Tar Heels in a game that seemed impossible to fritter away.

"I couldn't believe it when it was happening," said Neill McGeachy, the stunned Duke coach. "I still can't believe it now. It's like a horror movie I keep replaying over and over in my mind in slow motion. And every time, it still ends the same way. We had an eight-point lead. We blew it. We lost."

The Blue Devils were the Atlantic Coast Conference cellar dwellers with a dismal 10–14 record going into that final regular season game. The only thing expected of them was that they show up for the regionally televised game in sold-out Carmichael Auditorium at Chapel Hill. North Carolina (20–3)—with future NBA stars Bobby Jones, Mitch Kupchak, and Walter Davis—was ranked fourth in the nation.

But Duke surprised everybody by playing the highly touted Tar Heels even throughout the game. The lead changed hands an amazing 27 times and was tied on 17 occasions. Then, with just 17 seconds left, underdog Duke forged ahead 86–78, sending the packed house of North Carolina fans into disbelieving shock.

When the Tar Heels' Bobby Jones was fouled and sank both free throws to make the score 86–80, the Blue Devils still looked like sure winners. All they had to do was inbound the ball and run out the clock.

But Walter Davis stole the inbounds pass and found teammate John Kuester alone under the basket for a lay-up that cut the lead to 86–82 with 13 seconds left.

Again Duke tried to put the ball in play. And again Davis leaped in and swiped the ball right out of the hands of the now gun-shy Blue Devils. Davis' shot from the sideline bounced off the rim, but Jones grabbed the rebound and scored. Duke now led 86–84 with six seconds remaining.

The Blue Devils finally were able to get the ball to Pete Kramer, who was promptly fouled. The Duke bench breathed a huge sigh of relief. With four seconds left, Kramer went to the line for a one-and-one. He could widen the two-point margin and finally put the game out of reach for good.

But Kramer missed the free throw. The Tar Heels snared the rebound and called their last time-out with three seconds remaining. The Blue Devils still owned the lead. But a cloud of doom hung heavy over the Duke huddle. McGeachy schemed frantically to preserve the victory, but, as he later admitted, "I had the sinking feeling we were going down the drain and there was nothing I could do about it."

When play resumed, McGeachy had his biggest men guarding Kupchak, who was inbounding for the Tar Heels. Kupchak managed to fire the ball to Davis at midcourt, who took two dribbles and threw up a desperation 30-foot shot that went into the basket just as the horn went off.

The jubilant North Carolina fans stormed onto the court and hugged the players. Coach Smith fought his way through the mob to get a look at the scoreboard. "My gosh, have we won or something?" Smith shouted. "I thought the score was tied."

It was: 86–86. But not for long.

After the court was cleared of fans, the overtime that followed was anticlimactic. North Carolina breezed to a 96–92 win over the dazed and demoralized Blue Devils.

"Those 17 seconds lasted an eternity," moaned McGeachy. "I thought they would never end. That was the worst day of my life."

It was also McGeachy's last day as head coach. He was replaced after a single season at the Duke helm.

FOOLISH TALK

Los Angeles Lakers fans were in shock when they tuned in to a local radio sports talk show hosted by Joe McConnell in 1990.

With veteran Lakers guards Byron Scott and Michael Cooper (shown in photo) appearing on the show, McConnell announced both had been traded to the lowly Los Angeles Clippers for Benoit Benjamin and rookie Jeff Martin.

After eight angry callers expressed their dismay over the one-sided deal, Lakers center Mychal Thompson phoned and said on the air, "Scott and Cooper won't be missed. Byron is overrated and Cooper is over the hill."

Only then did McConnell remind listeners of what day it was— April Fools' Day.

Andrew D. Bernstein/NBA Photos

COLGATE RED RAIDERS

Dec. 6, 1986

The Colgate Red Raiders found a way to lose that was simply timeless.

With one second left in a tie game, the Red Raiders were hit with a technical foul for calling a time-out when they didn't have any time-outs left. The free throw broke the deadlock and sent Colgate to its 23rd straight defeat.

"We almost won," recalled former Colgate coach Joe Baker. "We could have won. We should have won. But we didn't. Our guys just forgot that we were out of time-outs and it cost us the game."

Colgate, a Division I team, was playing in the 1986 Hofstra Tournament. With the smaller Division II Franklin and Marshall Diplomats as its opponent, Baker was sure the victory-starved Red Raiders would finally notch a win and save face. But they ended up red-faced instead.

With five seconds remaining, Colgate was ahead 71–69 when Franklin and Marshall called a time-out to set up a last-ditch shot. But just as play was about to resume, Baker then called his team's final time-out to give his own squad more time to plot its defense.

"The game was almost over and it looked like we might win one—finally," recalled Baker. "After we called the time-out I warned my players it was our last one. I guess in all the excitement, they just forgot."

The Diplomats ran their play perfectly by splitting the Red Raiders' defense and scoring a lay-up that tied the game at 71–71 with one second left to play.

Immediately, all five Colgate players—forgetting what their coach had told them—yelled for time at the same moment. To Baker's utter dismay, the refs stopped the clock—and then signaled a technical foul on Colgate for calling an illegal time-out.

"Our players had been warned, but in a tight game and in the heat of the moment, the normal thing is to stop play," the coach said.

Baker and his boys watched helplessly as Franklin and Marshall connected on the free throw, then inbounded the ball, and ran out the final second. The Red Raiders walked solemnly off the court after the heartbreaking 72–71 loss.

"What a terrible way to lose," sighed Baker. "It made it even tougher that we almost broke our embarrassing losing streak but didn't."

The Red Raiders lost eight more games, extending their losing string to 31 straight defeats before finally beating Manhattanville a month later. But the victory could not erase the painful memory of the game that they had lost in no time at all.

FRED SNOWDEN

Coach ○ University of Arizona Wildcats ○ Jan. 9, 1982

In his final year as head coach, Fred Snowden suffered a technical knockout.

He had just announced that he was retiring at the end of the 1982 season when the Washington State Cougars arrived in Tucson to play his Arizona Wildcats. He should have packed his bags and left early. In the final second of play, Snowden was anything but retiring, and his shameful behavior cost the Wildcats a victory they already had locked up.

With a 53–51 lead, possession of the ball, and only 13 seconds left in the game, Arizona was poised to start celebrating. But instead of playing it safe, Snowden signaled the Wildcats to go for one more shot.

Guard Jeff Collins drove the lane and was called for charging WSU's Craig Ehlo. The Cougars' guard hit the first of the one-and-one but missed the second. However, WSU center Aaron Haskins was fouled as he pulled down the rebound. Haskins hit both ends of his one-and-one, putting the Cougars on top by a point, 54–53, with ten seconds left.

By now Snowden was pacing the sidelines, livid over the foul calls and screaming invectives at the refs.

The Cougars' hard press on Arizona in the backcourt didn't help Snowden's blood pressure. The excitable coach nearly collapsed when one of his guards, freshman Bronk Brunkhorst, was called for stepping on the boundary line.

Washington State took over with one tick left on the clock. The inbounds pass went to Tyrone Brown, who was intentionally fouled by Brunkhorst.

At that point, the simmering Snowden boiled over. He jerked loose from the assistant coaches, who were trying to restrain him, and charged onto the court. Snowden angrily protested that Brown had charged into Brunkhorst and that Arizona should get the ball back with one more chance to score.

The referee instantly signaled a technical against the coach for leaving the bench. But Snowden continued yelling at the officials and the second "T" went up. Then, before his assistants could drag Snowden off the floor, he was hit with a third technical for inciting the crowd.

The trio of "T's" meant automatic ejection for Snowden, but by then it was all over anyway. Brown went to the line and shot eight straight free throws—two for the intentional foul and six bonuses for Snowden's tantrum.

Brown made five of the eight shots and the Cougars, who had been losing by two with 13 seconds to go, racked up five points in the final second to win 59–53.

After he calmed down, Snowden admitted that his mortifying emotional outburst had cost his team dearly.

"I thought we had the game won," Snowden said. "I don't know what happened. I just lost it out there. It was a terribly embarrassing way to close out a coaching career."

SOUTH CAROLINA GAMECOCKS

Feb. 20, 1988

South Carolina was enjoying a 14-point lead over Louisville with about a minute to go. But the Gamecocks then lost their heads—and the game.

Rather than play out the waning moments and coast to victory, South Carolina triggered a 20-minute bench-clearing brawl that featured a wrestling match on top of the scorer's table. When the feathers stopped flying, four players and the Gamecocks' coach were ejected.

Thanks to a series of technical fouls called against South Carolina, the Cardinals scored six points without using up a single second. Louisville then tied the game in regulation and won in double overtime.

"I guess that shows anything can happen," Cardinals coach Denny Crum said in an understatement.

Louisville (15–9) looked like it was headed for its tenth defeat of the year, trailing the Gamecocks (14–8) by 14 points with slightly more than a minute to play at Carolina Coliseum.

At the 1:06 mark, Cardinals freshman guard LaBradford Smith hit a three-pointer, cutting the deficit to 72–61. No one thought it mattered because no one doubted the outcome.

But before the scorekeeper could even put the points on the board, a fight broke out between the two centers, South Carolina's Darryl Martin and Louisville's Purvis Ellison. Martin was called for a foul. Then Smith and Gamecocks guard Terry Gould began throwing fists. Other players jumped in and the free-for-all was on.

In the midst of the melee, Martin and Cardinals forward Herb Crook wrestled atop the scorer's table while coaches and officials struggled to separate the other brawlers.

And just when peace had been almost restored, a fan leaped across the scorer's table and started punching Crook.

"I was trying to peel Herb off the South Carolina player when this guy came out of the stands and hit Herb at least two times on the head," recalled Louisville's sports information director Kenny Klein. "The guy had been taunting Louisville players the whole game."

The police grabbed the spectator and carted him off to jail. While Crook sat stunned on the floor nursing a bloody nose, the refs called a technical on the Gamecocks for the fan's assault on the Louisville player.

That technical, added to two others which were assessed against South Carolina for fighting, meant that Gamecocks coach George Felton had to go. NCAA rules state that the coach is ejected after three technical fouls are called against his team—even if they're not on him personally.

But Felton had plenty of fellow ejectees to keep him company. The Gamecocks' Martin and Gould and the Cardinals' Smith and Crook also earned early showers and technicals for fighting.

After the 20-minute row subsided, Ellison went to the line and hit two free throws for the foul that had been called when Martin's shove started the fisticuffs.

Louisville's Kenny Payne then stepped to the charity stripe and made four of six for the three technicals called against South Carolina. But the Gamecocks' Terry Dozier, a 74 percent foul shooter, missed three of the four free throws awarded for the two technicals called against the Cardinals.

The game clock still read 1:06. But instead of having a 72–61 lead, South Carolina now led by only 73–67. Then, with 45 seconds to go, Ellison hit a jumper. At 0:27, teammate Felton Spencer was fouled and made both free throws to bring the Cardinals to within two points, 73–71. With four seconds left, the Gamecocks' Dozier was fouled. The team's high-point man missed one of his two free throws, but the 74–71 margin still seemed big enough.

It wasn't. Louisville's Craig Hawley swished a 33-foot three-point fling-and-a-prayer at the buzzer and sent the game into overtime. Both teams stayed even during the first extra period. But in the second overtime, the coachless Gamecocks came undone and lost 98–88.

Ellison credited the brawl with igniting the Cardinals' comeback victory. "The fight helped us out a lot," he said. "Until it happened, I thought the game was over and we had lost."

A remorseful Martin, who triggered the costly fray, blamed himself for the woeful windup. Muttered Martin, "With only a minute to play, we would have won if I had kept my head on straight."

MILWAUKEE BUCKS
Nov. 18, 1972

Leading by a huge 86–68 margin with under six minutes to play, the Milwaukee Bucks were bounding to an easy win over the stumbling New York Knicks.

But in the end it was Milwaukee that took the biggest pratfall. Unbelievably, the Knicks ran off 19 straight points while the Bucks went scoreless down the stretch. As a result, Milwaukee succumbed 87–86 in the NBA's most atrociously blown game ever.

What was so amazing was that the Bucks squandered their 18-point lead so late in the game with an all-star lineup of shot makers such as Kareem Abdul-Jabbar, Oscar Robertson, Bobby Dandridge, and Lucius Allen.

While a standing-room-only crowd of 19,694 Madison Square Garden fans suffered in silence, Milwaukee was coasting to a seemingly safe 86–68 lead at the 5:50 mark in the fourth quarter. Then Abdul-Jabbar, the game's high scorer, went up for an easy dunk—and bounced the ball off the rim and over the backboard. That was a portent of things to come.

For the first time in the game, the partisan crowd had something to cheer about. And when the Knicks scored the next five points, the fans roared, yelled, and stamped their feet. The noise level cranked up to ear-splitting decibels that clearly rattled the Bucks, who then called time-out with 4:15 left.

"When Kareem bounced the ball off the rim, that really got the crowd into the game," recalled Milwaukee coach Larry Costello. "We had them quiet up to that point, but when the place went wild, our guys just panicked."

Blowing the game then became a total team effort. After Kareem muffed the dunk, the rest of the Bucks lost their shooting touch—and composure.

After a New York basket cut the margin to 86–75 at the 3:30 mark, Robertson went in unguarded for a two-handed lay-up—and the ball skipped across the basket like it had a lid on it. Kareem missed on the rebound. Robertson, the game's most sure-handed guard, then fumbled the ball away.

And while the Bucks were self-destructing, the wobbly Knicks suddenly came off the ropes and couldn't miss. Earl Monroe and Walt Frazier started hitting and eventually combined for 17 of New York's final 19 points.

Seeing the panic in their opponents' eyes, the Knicks relentlessly chipped away at the lead. Reeling Milwaukee called another time-out to regroup with the score 86–81 and 2:03 left to play. Costello could barely make himself heard over the roar of the crowd as fans stood in their seats, screaming "Dee-fense! Dee-fense!"

The staggering Bucks were snakebit. Following the time-out, Dandridge immediately missed an easy lay-up, grabbed his own rebound—and blew the shot again. After a New York basket, Kareem missed another hook shot and Robertson missed from the outside.

Milwaukee's once gigantic lead was trimmed to one point, 86–85, as Frazier sank two free throws with 45 seconds on the clock. When Robertson tried to inbound the ball, Frazier fouled Allen. For the first time in the fatal six minutes, the Bucks breathed a sigh of relief. In a tight spot, there was nobody they would rather have at the line than Lucius Allen, one of the NBA's deadliest free throw shooters.

Incredibly, Allen missed both freebies! The Knicks got the ball back and Monroe canned a basket with 36 seconds left, sending his team into an 87–86 lead—and sending the crowd into delirium.

Milwaukee still had plenty of time to regain the lead. But Kareem missed another patented skyhook. New York's Dave DeBusschere grabbed the rebound and shoveled the ball out to Bill Bradley with 26 seconds left. With a one-point edge, Bradley tried to dribble out the clock—and almost went home wearing the goat horns. He had lost track of the time and was called for a 24-second violation.

The Bucks now had two seconds left for a last gasp chance to avoid the disgrace. The ball went to Kareem for the final shot. But Kareem, who had already scored 32 points in the game, threw up an air ball from the baseline. The game was over; the collapse was complete.

Following the stunning loss, a shellshocked Costello sat staring into space in a corner of the dressing room. "I thought we'd beat them good," he mumbled. "The Knicks were struggling. They were ready to fold. Then bingo! We had a complete collapse. If they had missed just one shot and we had gotten the rebound, or if we'd made one shot or a couple of free throws, it's over."

In another corner of the room, the Bucks' Jon McGlocklin shook his head in disbelief. "I was on the bench watching," he recalled, "and I kept saying, 'This is ridiculous. There's no way they can catch us.' The next thing I know the game was over and we'd lost."

Even the victorious Knicks were in awe of Milwaukee's spectacular collapse. "This just doesn't happen," said an incredulous Walt

Frazier. "Even if you have ten men on the court, you can't hold the Bucks scoreless for that long."

Back in Milwaukee, where the game was televised, Costello's wife, Barbara, did what many Bucks fans felt like doing—she kicked the TV set. "I couldn't believe what I'd just seen," she explained.

"I can't explain it," shrugged Costello. "It was unbelievable. Call it a jinx. Call it any damn thing you want."

Call it the most shamefully blown game in NBA history.

WHO ELSE BELONGS IN THE BASKETBALL HALL OF SHAME?

Do you have any nominations for *The Basketball Hall of SHAME?* Give us your picks for the most shameful, funny, embarrassing, wacky, boneheaded moments in hoops history. Here's your opportunity to pay a light-hearted tribute to the game we all love.

Please describe your nominations in detail. Those nominations that are documented with the greatest number of facts—such as firsthand accounts, newspaper or magazine clippings, box scores, or photos—have the best chance of being inducted into *The Basketball Hall of SHAME.* Feel free to make up your own categories and send as many nominations as you wish. All submitted material becomes the property of *The Basketball Hall of SHAME* and is nonreturnable. Mail your nominations to:

The Basketball Hall of SHAME
P.O. Box 31867
Palm Beach Gardens, FL 33420

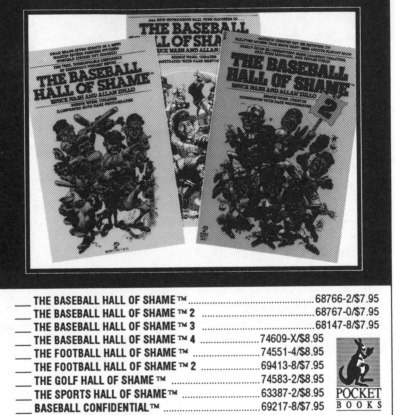